Peru

Peru

by Marion Morrison

Enchantment of the World™
Second Series

Children's Press®

An Imprint of Scholastic Inc.

New York Toronto London Auckland Sydney
Mexico City New Delhi Hong Kong
Danbury, Connecticut

Frontispiece: An Aymara woman in a traditional reed boat

Consultant: Richard Abisla, International Observer, Civic Council of Grassroots and
Indigenous Groups of Honduras

Please note: All statistics are as up-to-date as possible at the time of publication.

Book production by Herman Adler

Library of Congress Cataloging-in-Publication Data

Morrison, Marion.
 Peru / by Marion Morrison.
    p. cm.—(Enchantment of the world. Second series)
 Includes bibliographical references and index.
  ISBN-13: 978-0-531-20654-6
  ISBN-10: 0-531-20654-8
 1. Peru—Juvenile literature. I. Title. II. Series.
 F3408.5.M67 2009
 985—dc22   2008040356

1 2 3 4 5 6 7 8 9 10 R 19 18 17 16 15 14 13 12 11 10   62

Acknowledgments

The author wishes to thank the following people and organizations, who were particularly helpful in the preparation of this book: in Peru, Patricia Pianezzi de Rodgerson, Carmen Azurín, the late Eduardo Ronalds, Lolita Ronalds, Eleanor Griffis de Zuniga of the *Peruvian Times*, and the staff of the National Library; in London, the cultural section of the Peruvian Embassy and the library of Canning House.

Contents

Cover photo:
Machu Picchu

Uros Islands

Peruvian girl

A Snapshot
of Peru

F OR MOST VISITORS, THE FIRST STOP IN PERU IS LIMA, THE nation's capital. It lies at the heart of a long desert that runs along Peru's coast. Lima is a huge, busy metropolis packed with churches, museums, and reminders of the nation's past. The city's rich history spans more than 4,000 years, from the time of ancient coastal and highland civilizations through the Inca Empire, conquest by Spain in the 16th century, and, finally, independence in the 19th century.

Opposite: **Plaza de Armas is at the heart of Lima, the capital of Peru.**

Cusco Cathedral was completed in 1654.

Cusco

The next stop for most tourists is the Inca capital of Cusco, a flight of about an hour from Lima. Cusco stands at nearly 11,000 feet (3,400 meters) above sea level. It takes a while for visitors to get used to the thin air. In Inca times, palaces surrounded the main square at the center of the city. Today, Cusco Cathedral and the Jesuit Church stand on the square. Many people consider the church to be the most beautiful in the city, with finely carved balconies and altars covered in gold leaf. Narrow cobblestone streets lined with Inca and Spanish buildings lead from the square.

The Church of Santo Domingo sits atop the Inca Temple of the Sun in Cusco.

When the Spanish conquered the Inca, they built their own churches and palaces on top of the Inca walls in Cusco. The Spanish Church of Santo Domingo, for instance, is built above the Inca Temple of the Sun, the most revered shrine of the Inca Empire. When great earthquakes shook the city, in 1650 and at other times, the Inca walls remained standing, while colonial and modern buildings collapsed.

PERU

- ● Cities of more than 150,000 people
- ○ Other cities
- ✪ National capital
- ∴ Archaeological site

0   200 miles

0   200 kilometers

COLOMBIA

ECUADOR

Pan-American Highway

Putumayo R.

Napo R.

Tigre R.

Iquitos

Amazon R.

BRAZIL

Tumbes

Marañón R.

Nauta

Yavari R.

Talara

Sullana

Requena

Paita

Piura

Marañón R.

Moyobamba

Yurimaguas

Laquipampa Reserved Zone

Chachapoyas

Tarapoto

Chiclayo

Cajamarca

Chaparrí Private Conservation Area

Río Abiseo National Park

Cordillera Azul National Park

Chan Chan

Trujillo

Salaverry

Santa Lucía

Huallaga R.

Pucallpa

Pan-American Highway

Yungay

Huaráz

Tingo María

Ucayali R.

Chimbote

Huascarán Nat'l Park

Huánuco

PACIFIC OCEAN

Cerro de Pasco

Urubamba R.

Interoceanic Highway

Alto Purus Nat'l Park

Huacho

Morococha

Mantaro R.

Huancayo

Otishi National Park

Manu Nat'l Park

Tambopata-Candamo Reserve

Puerto Maldonado

Callao

Lima

Huancavelica

Quillabamba

Machu Picchu

Bahuaja-Sonene Nat'l Park

BOLIVIA

Pisco

Ayacucho

Abancay

Cusco

Ica

Interoceanic Highway

Nazca Lines

Nazca

Cailloma

Juliaca

Lake Titicaca

San Juan

Yauca

Interoceanic Highway

Puno

Arequipa

Desaguadero

Pan-American Highway

Matarani

Mollendo

Moquegua

Ilo

Tacna

Lake Poopó

CHILE

Peru

Machu Picchu

Many visitors next head to Machu Picchu, the so-called Lost City of the Incas. Machu Picchu is set on a stunning site, high on a mountainside surrounded by the craggy peaks of the Andes Mountains. The Machu Picchu ruins include temples, palaces, houses, courtyards, prisons, and fountains. The Inca people cut steps into the mountainsides below the city so they would have flat land on which to grow crops. Today, these agricultural terraces still step spectacularly down the slopes.

A llama near Machu Picchu

This colorful macaw lives in the Amazon rain forest.

The Amazon Forest

A quick flight of less than an hour takes visitors to Peru's Amazon rain forest. The lowlands are a completely different world than the cool, misty forests of the mountains. Here, it is hot and rains frequently, and the world is alive with animals. Sometimes, hundreds of brilliantly colored macaws, birds that belong to the parrot family, crowd together along a riverbank.

In the Clouds

Back in Cusco, a train carries travelers south toward Lake Titicaca, the world's highest navigable lake. The journey across the high plains, or *altiplano*, takes all day and reaches its highest point at La Raya, 14,202 feet (4,329 m) above sea level, not far from towering Andean peaks.

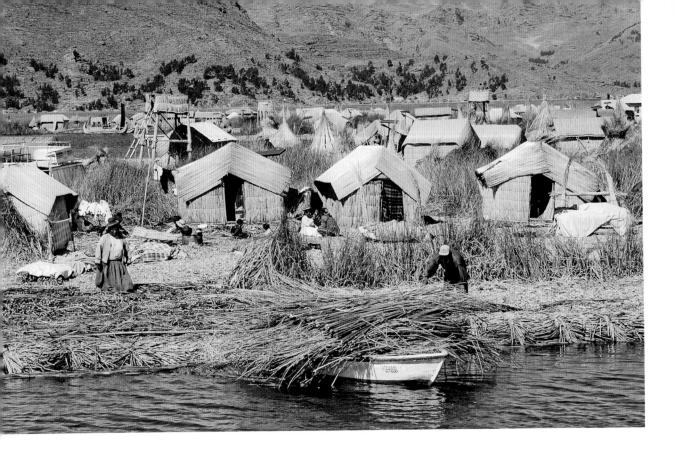

Some Aymara people live on islands made of reeds in Lake Titicaca.

The Andes and the high plains are home to Peru's largest indigenous, or native, groups, the Quechua and the Aymara. Some Aymara live on islands in Lake Titicaca and still use traditional boats made of reeds. The lake, which is surrounded by towering, snowcapped mountains, is a stunning sight, shimmering far into the distance like an inland sea.

Arequipa and the Nazca Lines

West from Lake Titicaca across southern Peru is the country's second-largest city, Arequipa, which sits at the foot of the El Misti volcano. Arequipa is a beautiful city with fine colonial buildings. From there, it is a short journey to the site of some of Peru's ancient civilizations.

People from one of these civilizations, the Nazca, made lines and drawings of animals—including a spider, a monkey, a whale, and birds—that cover a large area of the desert around their valley. Since the lines were discovered in the 1920s, many people have tried to explain their significance. One German mathematician spent more than 50 years in the desert making calculations relating the lines to stars. Other experts have used computers and researched indigenous spiritual thinking to find an explanation. But, to date, no one has solved the mystery.

These are just a few of the intriguing sights and diverse landscapes of Peru. From desert to mountains to rain forest to cities, Peru is a country that amazes.

The Nazca people created huge drawings in the Peruvian desert. The drawings were made between about 100 BCE and 500 CE.

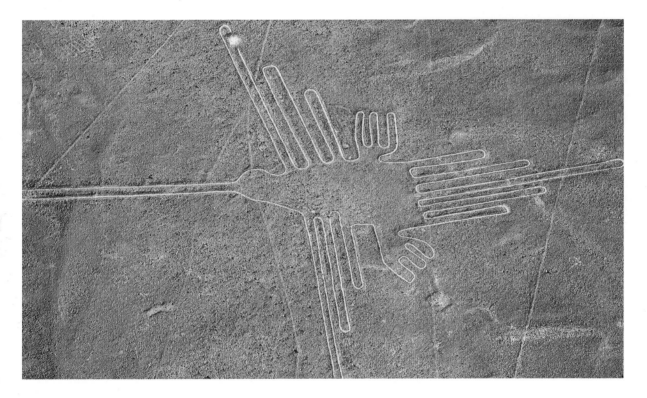

Mountain, Desert, and Rain Forest

The Gálvez River is one of the many tributaries of the Amazon.

Peru, the third-largest country in South America after Brazil and Argentina, is a land of extremes. Several icy peaks in the Andes Mountains tower more than 4 miles (6 kilometers) high above sandy deserts. The great Amazon River begins in the mountains of Peru, and 60 percent of the country is a damp tropical forest that spreads out around the Amazon and its tributaries. The country also has active volcanoes, shimmering lakes, and lush valleys filled with farms.

Peru lies on the west coast of South America. It borders the Pacific Ocean to the west, Ecuador to the north, Colombia to the northeast, Brazil to the east, Bolivia to the southeast, and Chile to the south. It covers an area of 496,222 square miles (1,285,209 sq km), making it almost twice the size of Texas.

Opposite: **The Andes is the highest mountain range outside of Asia. Its peaks have an average height of about 13,000 feet (4,000 m).**

Peru's Geographic Features

Highest Elevation:
Mount Huascarán, 22,205 feet
(6,768 m) above sea level

Lowest Elevation: Sea level,
along the Pacific Coast

Area: 496,222 square miles
(1,285,209 sq km)

**Greatest Distance North to
South:** 1,225 miles (1,971 km)

Greatest Distance East to West:
854 miles (1,374 km)

Longest Shared Border:
1,803 miles (2,901 km), with
Colombia

Largest Lake: Titicaca, 3,232
square miles (8,371 sq km) on
the border of Peru and Bolivia

Highest Lake: Titicaca, 12,507
feet (3,812 m) above sea level

Average High Temperatures:

	January	July
Lima	82°F (28°C)	66°F (19°C)
Cusco	68°F (20°C)	70°F (21°C)
Iquitos	90°F (32°C)	88°F (31°C)

Lowest Annual Precipitation:
Less than 1 inch (2.5 cm),
in Lima

Highest Annual Precipitation:
More than 100 inches (250 cm),
in Iquitos

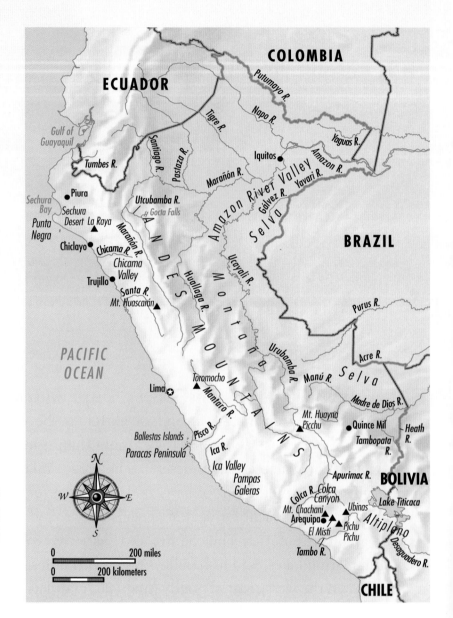

The Long Desert

Desert extends almost the full length of Peru's coastline. Though the desert is more than 1,000 miles (1,600 km) long, it is only about 10 to 100 miles (16 to 160 km) wide. Lima, Peru's capital, is in the center of this long desert. Lima and other parts of the desert are frequently covered with a thick, gray fog.

In the north, the Sechura Desert has shifting sands, scrub forests, and shallow lakes. Few people live in the Sechura, but some people work there mining phosphate rock to make fertilizer. The central and southern parts of the desert are a mix of vast sand dunes and barren, rocky land. Farther south, parts of the desert slope gently inland to higher altitudes, reaching 7,557 feet (2,303 m) near Arequipa, Peru's second-largest city.

Rippled sand dunes mark the desert near Casma, on the north-central coast.

The Peru Current

As the first European explorers sailed toward Peru, they found the Pacific Ocean unusually cool and often shrouded in mist. Yet the nearby coastal land was desert, receiving almost no rain. In 1802, a German scientist named Alexander von Humboldt checked the temperature of the ocean off the Peruvian coast. He found that it was about 8 degrees Fahrenheit (4.5° Celsius) lower than the temperature in places at a similar latitude (distance from the equator) elsewhere on the planet. Scientists have since discovered that the cold current rises from a deep ocean trench close to the shore.

Humboldt also found that the air temperature over the land was warmer than it was over the ocean. He had, in fact, discovered one of the conditions that created the desert, but it was many years before this was understood.

Normally, wind blowing in from the ocean is warm and moist. It cools over the land, condenses, and then releases rain. Along Peru's coastal desert, however, the wind from the ocean is cool. As it blows over the land, the wind warms. And because warm air can hold more moisture than cold air, it draws moisture from the land.

This condition creates a desert often shrouded in fog, but where it hardly ever rains.

Peru's cold ocean currents were long known as the Humboldt Current, but today they are often called the Peru Current.

Many rivers flow from the Andes Mountains into the Pacific Ocean. They cut across the long desert, creating valleys. Farmers have been cultivating these valleys for centuries. Some of these valleys, such as the Chicama in the north and the Ica in the south, are broad and fertile. Others are little more than rocky gorges where plants cling to damp soil.

The Andes

The Andes Mountains, the highest mountain chain outside of Asia, form the backbone of Peru. The country's tallest peak, Mount Huascarán, crowns the central chain at 22,205 feet (6,768 m).

The mountains are young in geological terms—only 40 million to 60 million years old. Earth's surface is divided into several huge pieces called tectonic plates. These plates are constantly moving in relation to one another. Over millions of years, mountain chains form in places where plates collide. The Andes were formed as the South American Plate pushed up over a plate under the Pacific Ocean. The borders of tectonic plates are also prone to earthquakes, and Peru suffers frequent quake tremors.

More than 30 peaks in Peru's Andes Mountains rise above 19,685 feet (6,000 m).

Deadly Quakes

Earthquakes are common in Peru, and some have been devastating. In 1970, an earthquake dislodged part of an ice sheet atop Mount Huascarán, causing an avalanche of mud, ice, and rock to sweep into the valley below. More than half the city of Huaraz was destroyed, and the town of Yungay completely disappeared. Only the tops of four palm trees that once stood in the main square were visible above the mud. About 70,000 people lost their lives in the earthquake.

On August 15, 2007, an earthquake flattened 80 percent of the coastal town of Pisco, a port about 125 miles (200 km) southeast of Lima. Some buildings in Pisco dated from the 1800s and had survived many tremors, but they could not take this one. Many people were attending mass in the San Clemente Cathedral when the quake hit, and 148 died when the roof collapsed. The earthquake killed a total of 430 people in the town.

The Peruvian Andes can be divided into three parts. The northern section is the lowest and the narrowest from east to west. The central section is a mass of high mountains with many snowcapped peaks. It includes the highest broad, fertile valleys and the main source of the Amazon River. Some parts of the central section are so rugged that a bus journey of 100 miles (160 km) takes all day. The mountains are broadest in the south section, stretching as far as 400 miles (650 km) east to west.

Most peaks in the western Andes are volcanic, including El Misti, which overlooks Arequipa, and Ubinas, Peru's most active volcano, which sometimes spews ash and rock.

Disappearing Glaciers

Many peaks in the Andes are covered with huge ice sheets called glaciers. But the glaciers in Peru's Andes are shrinking, and some seem destined to disappear within a few years. They are disappearing because the world's climate is changing as a result of global warming. Burning coal to run factories and using oil to power cars spews pollutants into the air. Some of these pollutants, called greenhouse gases, stay in the atmosphere, trapping the heat near the ground. This activity has raised global temperatures and altered the climate.

Scientists have been studying the Qori Kalis Glacier, which lies at 18,600 feet (5,700 m) above sea level in southeastern Peru. Qori Kalis is the world's largest tropical glacier. Since 1963, when scientists first measured the glacier, it has receded by 0.7 mile (1.1 km).

The Ausangate Glacier has shrunk so much that the Quechua people no longer hold their annual festival in which they climb the mountain to collect sacred ice to offer the mountain spirits. As the glacier slims, people in nearby communities are fearful for their future because they have long depended on the glacier for water for their crops. The mountains typically have distinct wet and dry seasons, and ancient mountain peoples built channels to carry precious water to their fields. Many of the channels are now dry for months on end because of the shrinking glaciers.

Looking at Peru's Cities

Arequipa (below), Peru's second-largest city, was home to nearly 750,000 people in 2007. The city, which was founded by the Spanish in 1540, is the chief trading center for southern Peru. Its main industries are textile manufacturing, soap production, and tourism. Because many of Arequipa's buildings are built from light-colored volcanic rock called *sillar*, the city is nicknamed the White City.

Peru's third-largest city, Trujillo, had a population of nearly 700,000 in 2007. Spaniard Diego de Almagro founded the city in 1534, naming it Villa Trujillo in honor of the Spanish town where Spanish conqueror Francisco Pizarro was born. These days, the city is the center of an agricultural region where much sugarcane and asparagus is produced.

Chiclayo (above), one of Peru's fastest-growing cities, was founded by Spanish priests in the 1560s. Today, it has a population of more than 500,000. Chiclayo is Peru's fourth-largest city and the commercial center of the northwest.

Small lakes dot the Peruvian Andes. Some, like those near Huascarán, lie in glacial valleys and are filled with milky blue water from glaciers. Others are merely shallow ponds in the valleys between mountain ranges.

Many rivers start high in the Andes. The Marañón and Ucayali rivers both rise in the Andes and flow for about 1,000 miles (1,600 km) before meeting in northwestern Peru to form the Amazon River.

Children enjoy swimming in the Marañón River.

The Altiplano

Between the southern Andean mountain ranges lies the *altiplano*, a relatively unbroken area of high plains. Much of this region slopes southward and drains into Lake Titicaca, the world's highest navigable lake, which lies on the Peru-Bolivia border. It is South America's largest freshwater lake, covering 3,232 square miles (8,371 sq km), twice the area of the U.S. state of Rhode Island.

Mountain, Desert, and Rain Forest   **25**

Clouds hang in ridges in the montaña.

The Montaña

East of the Andes lies the humid Amazon forest. Much of the forested area is mountainous and is known as the *montaña*. On the eastern side of the mountains, typical mountain vegetation of grasses and small plants extends downward to about 8,200 feet (2,500 m). At this point, the grasses give way to low bushes and shrubs. This line is known as the *ceja de la montaña*—literally, the "eyebrow of the mountain"—and it marks the point where moisture and warmth rising from the Amazon forest below allow richer growth.

Many valleys, swift rivers, canyons, and high waterfalls break up the lush montaña. Close to the foot of the Andes, some rivers are almost 1 mile (1.6 km) wide. Most are shallow and follow a meandering course through the forests heading northeast toward the Amazon River.

Gocta Falls

Gocta Falls tumbles a total of 2,532 feet (772 m) over limestone cliffs in the Amazon region of northeastern Peru. It is one of the world's highest waterfalls, but until 2005, only local people knew about it. Its existence was announced to the rest of the world after an expedition by a group of Peruvian and German explorers. The falls are surrounded by pristine cloud forest—forest almost permanently shrouded in clouds. This cloud forest is home to many rare creatures, including the critically endangered yellow-tailed woolly monkey, of which only an estimated 250 remain, and the marvelous spatuletail, a tiny hummingbird that gets its name from its very long tail feathers. The Gocta Falls region is also home to gray-breasted mountain toucans; scarlet-fronted parakeets; and torrent ducks, which can survive in fast-flowing streams and rivers.

The Selva

The low-lying area around the Amazon River is called the *selva*, meaning "jungle." The forested lowlands of the selva are the least-developed region of Peru. Iquitos, the largest city in the region, with a population of nearly 400,000, lies on the Amazon. It can be reached only by air or river because no roads cut through the thick forest. In most of the selva, riverboats or canoes are the only form of transportation. In the dry season, sandbanks and fallen trees make river travel hazardous.

Canoes are used for transportation in the thick jungles near the Amazon.

Climate

Peru is a country of many environments and many climates. The coastal desert has a mild climate, with average high temperatures generally ranging from 66°F (19°C) to 82°F (28°C) throughout the year. In the mountains, temperatures rise to about 70°F (21°C) during the warmest months. The Amazon region is hot and humid year-round, with temperatures often reaching above 90°F (32°C).

Thick clouds hang over Machu Picchu. Downpours are common there from December to March.

Rain seldom falls in the central or southern parts of the coastal desert, although central areas are covered in fog for many months of the year. Most rain falls in the mountains from November through April. The western and southern ranges tend to be drier. Snowfall is common above 16,500 feet (5,000 m).

On the eastern side of the Andes and in the Amazon lowlands, rain may fall almost any time of the year, although November through March are usually the wettest months and June through September the driest. The total amount of rain varies greatly. At Quince Mil, on the heavily forested eastern Andean slope, the annual rainfall sometimes reaches 26 feet (8 m).

Sometimes, cold winds from the south sweep through the southern parts of the rain forest. The average temperature in the Amazonian city of Puerto Maldonado is 79°F (26°C) throughout the year, but with these frigid winds, the temperature can fall as low as 46°F (8°C) for several days.

Magnificent Life

PERU IS AN EXTRAORDINARY LAND FILLED WITH EXTRAOR-dinary life. The Amazon forest has more plant and animal species than any other place on Earth. Although this forest spreads through nine countries, Peru likely has the highest number of species of any of them. The reason is simple. The forest does not stop at the foot of the Andes Mountains. Instead, it spreads up the eastern slopes. The types of trees and other plants change according to altitude, creating different habitats for animals. The Amazon forest also extends more than 1,000 miles (1,600 km) southward through Peru, producing a variety of climates with the changes in latitude. This, too, affects the plant and animal life that survives there.

So many different species exist in Peru that scientists have not yet identified and counted them all. As settlers and developers clear land and destroy forest habitats, some species could disappear before the scientists' task is complete.

Opposite: **A three-toed sloth clings to a tree in the Amazon forest.**

Green anacondas are the largest snakes in the Amazon forest.

Magnificent Life **31**

Life Along the Coast

Many cactuses grow in Peru's desert coast. Prickly pear cactuses have edible fruit and flat, rounded paddles covered with spines. They grow mostly along the edges of valleys, where they are often used as fences. The slender, columnlike San Pedro cactus is another common Peruvian cactus. Native peoples have used it as medicine for at least 2,000 years.

Cactuses are common along Peru's desert coast.

In Peru's coastal valleys, low trees with deep roots can find footholds in dry riverbeds. Most are pod-bearing trees such as the algarrobo, which produces seeds used in medicine. Many kinds of small mimosas plants also grow in this region, including the sensitive mimosa, whose leaves fold tightly when touched.

In a few parts of the coast, the dense fog sometimes condenses into water. In these moist areas, known as *lomas*, trees can grow.

Moisture condensing on tree leaves drips to the ground, giving life to a green carpet of mosses and ferns below. The lomas are home to many species of birds not normally seen in the desert, including doves, plovers, cuckoos, and the tiny vermillion flycatcher.

Monkeys, deer, and some sloths live in the northern coastal valleys. Foxes and small rodents live in the desert region, but the desert's largest mammals are restricted to the seashore. Tens of thousands of seals and sea lions live along the coast. Some rocky places are so crowded that there is hardly a square inch of empty space.

The brightly colored head of the male Andean cock-of-the-rock helps it attract mates.

A Rare Bird

The white-winged guan is a turkeylike bird found only in Peru. It lives in the dry scrub forests of the northwest, feeding on fruit, flowers, and seeds. Most plants in this region grow slowly, so if the land is cleared, it takes a long time for them to regrow. As these forests have been destroyed, the white-winged guan has become severely endangered. Fewer than 250 of them survive today. Two protected areas, the Laquipampa Reserved Zone and the Chaparrí Private Conservation Area, have been set aside to give the birds a chance to live and breed in some of the region's remaining untouched forest.

Millions of cormorants, pelicans, gannets, and other seabirds live on the coast and on islands such as the Ballestas, near Pisco, south of Lima. The birds dive into the sea for fish with pinpoint accuracy.

Pelicans rest on a rocky outcrop along the coast.

Life in the Mountains

In northern Peru, the climate is wetter than in the south, and the mountainsides are green. In this region, small plants grow close to the ground, while some larger species survive in the valleys. Most western slopes of the central and southern mountains are treeless. Slow-growing trees, largely of the rose family, stood here at one time, but most have been cut down in the last 500 years. Relics of the forests exist in a few isolated places, and some are now protected. The most prominent trees today are the tall eucalyptus trees, which were introduced from Australia more than a century ago. The puya raimondi, a low plant that shoots out a huge stalk of flowers, also grows in this region.

The National Flower

Peru's national flower is a long, brightly colored tubular flower called the cantuta. This flower has a special place in the folklore of the Quechua people of the Andes Mountains, who use it in funeral rites.

Grasslands cover the higher mountain slopes. Animal life here is sparse. Several small rodents, including the guinea pig, are native to the Andes. Most birds in this region are also small. The Andean flicker, a type of woodpecker, nests in the sides of dry riverbeds. The master of the skies is the giant Andean condor, a vulture with a wingspan of 10 feet (3 m). Condors nest on rocky mountain ledges and soar around the mountaintops or fly to the coast, where they feed on dead seals and other dead animals.

A Giant Flower

Pineapples and yuccas belong to the bromeliads family of plants. Bromeliads have leaves that grow in a spiral formation, enabling them to collect water. The world's largest bromeliad is the puya raimondi. It grows only in a few parts of the Andes, including on the rugged slopes of central Peru, where scattered groups stand out against the yellow mountain grasses.

This huge bromeliad produces a flower stalk up to 33 feet (10 m) tall. Even the leafy lower part of the plant is taller than the average human. The leaves are tough, with sharp spines along the edges. These spines snare unwary predators, such as hawks hunting the small birds that nest in the plant.

The puya raimondi takes many years to develop. Once it matures, the flower spike shoots upward in a matter of months. More than 8,000 tiny flowers bearing feathery light seeds cover the central column. The puya raimondi flowers just once and then dies.

Common domestic animals in the Andes are llamas and alpacas. Llamas are members of the camel family. People who settled around Lake Titicaca domesticated llamas as long ago as 6,000 years. Llamas are kept for their meat and wool and are also used for carrying light loads. The alpaca, a slightly smaller cousin of the llama, is kept largely for its wool. The llama has two wild relatives—the vicuña, which lives in high grasslands, and the guanaco, which survives in the southern highlands.

A Quechua boy watches over his family's alpacas.

Back from Extinction

The vicuña, Peru's national animal, is the smallest of the Andean camel relatives. A fully grown male vicuña is little more than 3 feet (90 centimeters) tall at the shoulder. The vicuña has a long neck, golden brown fleece, and pointed ears.

Vicuña wool has been used for weaving since Inca times. The Inca people protected the animals. They rounded up and sheared them each year, and then afterward, they returned the creatures to the wild. The Inca allowed only a few women to work with the wool, which they turned into incredibly soft garments for Inca nobles to wear.

In the 20th century, hunters killed so many vicuñas illegally for their valuable wool that the animals were almost wiped out. In the 1960s, Peru created reserves where vicuñas could be protected. One important reserve is at Pampas Galeras, in the mountains above Nazca in southern Peru. New laws made it illegal to kill a vicuña. The measures were successful, and vicuñas are thriving once again.

Life in the Amazon Lowlands

The enormous selva in the Amazon lowlands is a wonderland of plants. Trees such as lapunas grow up to 150 feet (45 m) high. Their tall, straight trunks have no branches except at the top, where they emerge from a surrounding canopy of leafy, lower trees. From the higher branches, long trailing vines called lianas stretch to the ground.

The canopy is rich with life. Lizards lounge, butterflies flit, and birds such as parrots and toucans forage for fruits and seeds. Down on the ground are mammals such as jaguars, small deer, and peccaries, which look like pigs. The largest forest mammals are tapirs, which can weigh as much as 500 pounds (230 kilograms). These relatives of rhinoceroses use their large snouts to grab the leaves of plants and trees. Some mammals live both on the ground and in trees, including porcupines, anteaters, and many kinds of monkeys. Giant otters, turtles, and caimans, which are related to the crocodile, live in the rivers that flow through the Amazon lowlands.

Brazilian tapirs are the largest wild land animals in South America. They have flexible snouts that help them grab hard-to-reach food.

Protecting the Amazon Forest

East of Cusco, the mountains slope abruptly to Amazon lowland. In just 75 miles (120 km) the elevation drops from more than 16,400 feet to 820 feet (5000 m to 250 m), and tiny streams born in the snows become massive rivers that eventually flow into the Amazon. In the higher elevations, the raucous cries of howler monkeys echo through the misty forests, while at lower elevations, meandering rivers flow through lush rain forests.

This region has an immense diversity of species. Within a small area near the Tambopata River live more than 600 species of birds, 127 amphibians, 91 mammals, 94 fish, and 1,230 butterflies. In a single 2.5-acre (1 ha) plot, scientists counted 150 species of trees.

The Healing Tree

The national tree of Peru is the cinchona. At least six species of cinchonas grow in Peru. The tree gets its name from the Countess of Chinchón, the wife of the viceroy (governor) of Peru. In 1638, the countess came down with malaria, a deadly disease spread by mosquito bites that is common in tropical regions. She was treated with a tea made from the bark of a cinchona tree, which contains quinine. The concoction helped cure her. Quinine, which is also now produced in factories, is an important medicine in treating malaria.

Peru took its first steps in helping protect this region in 1967, when it created Manú National Park, which is centered on the Manú River, an Amazon tributary. In the 1970s, the government made the forests around the Tambopata River, another tributary, a reserve. More land was protected in the 1990s.

Perhaps the greatest threat to the region is the Interoceanic Highway, which connects Cusco with the Brazilian Amazon. The road follows the Tambopata River and is bringing more people and activity to the area, which could threaten the environment. Already, gold prospectors are working on some rivers, and in one area, illegal logging has destroyed the forest. Many people fear that if Peru does not do more to protect the plants and animals in the reserve, its amazing diversity will disappear.

Brightly colored macaws are among the many species that live in Manú National Park.

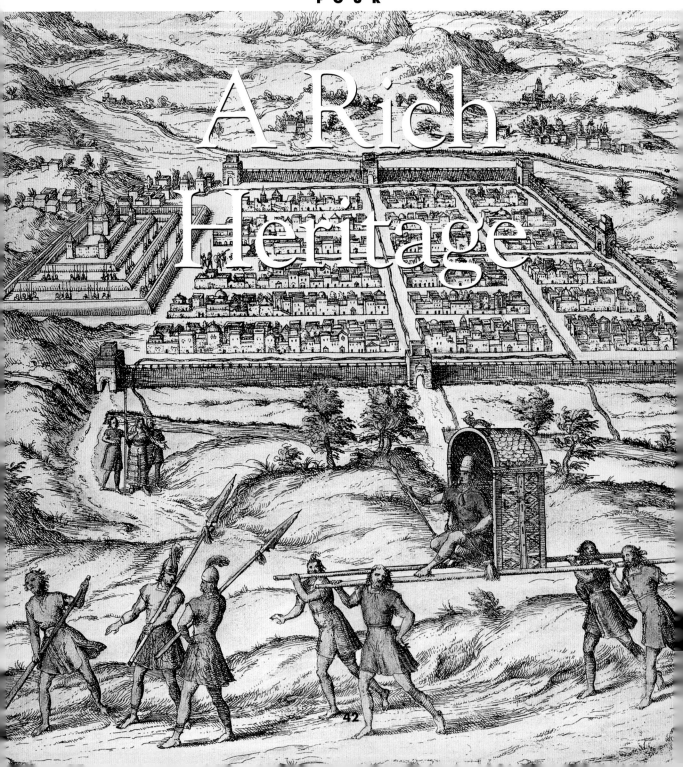

A Rich Heritage

Early people in Peru made fantastic stone carvings at Sechín, about 170 miles (270 km) north of Lima. The carvings depict warriors and fearsome heads.

THE FIRST PEOPLES TO LIVE IN PERU WERE NOMADIC hunters, gatherers, and fishers. Their ancestors probably arrived in North America from Asia, crossing dry land that connected areas that are now Russia and Alaska during the last ice age, when the seas were lower. Gradually, people spread across North and South America. By about 3000 BCE, they had settled in Peru's desert valleys, where they grew cotton and corn, and in the mountains, where they grew potatoes and grains.

Ancient Civilizations

Many centuries later, the descendants of these early peoples produced fine weavings and pots and built large ceremonial centers. The Chavín culture, which had settlements in the Andes 10,000 feet (3000 m) above sea level, dates from around 900 BCE. At Chavín de Huántar, the people of the Chavín culture built temples of massive stone blocks and decorated them with images of cats.

Opposite: **This engraving of people living in the Inca city of Cusco was made in 1572.**

Ancient Sites

Archaeologists have discovered the remains of several ancient civilizations in Peru. The Caral site, in the desert of Peru's Norte Chico region, includes pyramids, temples, plazas, and residences. Dating back to about 3000 BCE, it is one of the oldest settlements in the Americas. At Sechín, on the coast, stone walls remain from one of the earliest large buildings in Peru. The walls feature carvings of warriors and gruesome heads.

In the 1920s, scientists exploring along the southern coast found more than 400 mummies from the Paracas culture dating back to about 600 BCE. The mummies were wrapped in very fine woven cloths. The Nazca people, who also lived on the southern coast, were fine weavers and potters. They made lines and large drawings of animals in the desert. Their culture flourished from about 100 BCE until about 500 CE.

The Moche ruled much of the northern coast of Peru from about 100 to 700 CE. They were skilled engineers, building roads and canals. They also built huge pyramids that served as religious centers. The Moche used more than 140 million adobe bricks to build the Pyramid of the Sun. They also excelled at pottery and jewelry making, producing exquisite ornaments of gold, silver, and precious stones.

Around 700 CE, the Moche culture declined because of a food shortage. Much of Peru then came under the influence of the highland Huari civilization. Huari culture was centered near the modern city of Ayacucho, about 300 miles (500 km) southeast of Lima. At the same time, the Tiahuanaco civilization controlled the area around Lake Titicaca. Their capital city of Tiahuanaco, which bordered the lake in Bolivia, was then the highest city in the Americas.

When the Huari civilization lost power around 1000 CE, the Chimú, then the strongest of the coastal

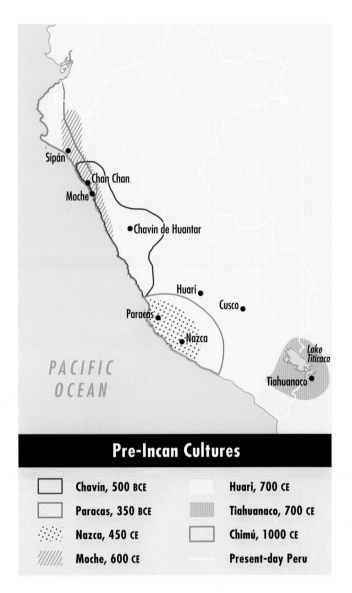

Pre-Incan Cultures

Chavín, 500 BCE		Huari, 700 CE	
Paracas, 350 BCE		Tiahuanaco, 700 CE	
Nazca, 450 CE		Chimú, 1000 CE	
Moche, 600 CE		Present-day Peru	

The Lord of Sipán

In 1987, archaeologists unearthed the burial tomb of a Moche leader called Lord of Sipán in the northern Peruvian desert. This was a particularly exciting discovery because, unlike most Moche tombs, this one was intact, almost untouched by grave robbers. This enabled archaeologists to see the exact position in which the Moche had buried the body. The tomb also contained the skeletons of young women, children, and warriors, along with gold, silver, and copper jewelry and other goods. Much of the treasure is now housed in the Royal Tombs of Sipán Museum in the city of Lambayeque.

peoples, developed into the largest empire in Peru. The Chimú capital was the mud-brick city of Chan Chan, on the northern coast near the modern city of Trujillo. Successive rulers built new quarters for themselves and their nobles, so the walled city became a massive maze of houses and passageways. At its height, Chan Chan was home to about 30,000 people. The Chimú created their empire with strong, well-disciplined armies. But they were no match for the Inca, who conquered them in the middle of the 15th century.

The Inca Empire

In the 1200s, the Inca were a small group in the Cusco region. Less than 300 years later, the Inca had defeated many other groups, creating the largest empire in the Americas. The capital of the empire was Cusco, a city the Inca filled with gold and silver.

The Inca built an extensive network of well-maintained roads. Along the roads were storehouses stocked with food and textiles that were used by the army or given to others during

Inca Empire

▪	Inca Empire by 1400	▪	added 1471–1493
▪	added 1400–1471	▪	added 1493–1525
—	Inca roads	—	Present-day borders

Inca Stonemasons

The Inca were expert stonemasons, and they carefully shaped massive blocks. The Inca did not use mortar, a paste that is generally used to fill in the gaps between blocks in stone walls. Instead, they fit the blocks together so carefully that it is impossible to pass a knife blade between them. Streets in Cusco are lined with walls made of the finely carved stone blocks, and people still marvel at a remarkable stone with twelve corners. One block in a fortress overlooking Cusco is believed to weigh more than 300 tons.

difficult years. The storehouses also fed the *chasquis,* or teams of runners who carried messages across the empire. The chasquis traveled approximately four times faster than a person on horseback because they could cross rope bridges and travel on narrow mountain paths where horses couldn't go.

The Inca people worked hard, and the empire generally cared for the sick and the elderly. Most people were farmers. They grew crops on the steep Andean slopes by cutting terraces into the hillsides to create flat plots of land and using irrigation to water the fields. The Inca's main crops were corn, potatoes, beans, and grains such as quinoa. Under a tax system called *mita,* everyone was obliged to do work for the empire, and farming was one way to fulfill this obligation.

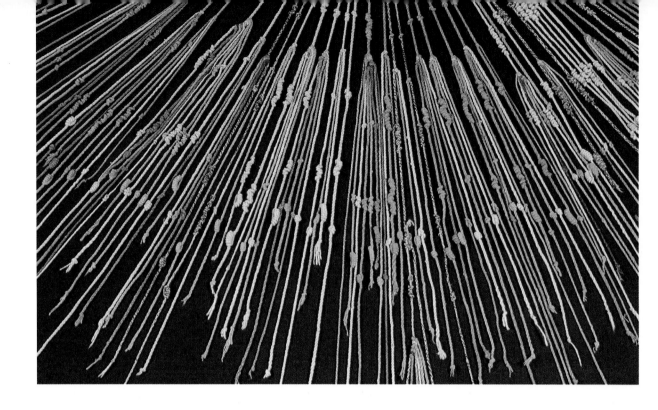

Quipus consisted of strings, often made of llama or alpaca hair. The knots in the strings represented numbers.

Other Inca worked as weavers, making clothing from llama wool and cotton. Inca clothing was simple. Both men and women wore sleeveless tunics with a cloak over their shoulders. A man's tunic was knee-length, while a woman's was ankle-length with a wide belt or sash at the waist. Inca cloth was sometimes brightly colored and patterned.

The Inca adopted Quechua from local tribes to use as a common language. They had no known form of writing, though they told stories that were passed down through generations, and patterns on woven cloth often told a story. To keep accounts and records, the Inca used a *quipu*, a device made of colored, knotted strings. Only experts could use and understand quipus.

By 1500, the Inca Empire stretched from an area that is now southern Colombia to central Chile. Because it was difficult to control such a large area, the Inca created a second capital in Quito, in what is now Ecuador. Inca ruler Huayna Capac moved to Quito because he was having trouble with northern tribes, but he died there in 1527 without having named an heir.

Who would take over the empire? The two leading contenders were his son, Huáscar, whom he had left in Cusco to look after that part of the empire, and Huáscar's half-brother Atahualpa, who had been with Huayna Capac in Quito. Civil war broke out between groups led by the brothers, and the empire fell into chaos.

Chachapoyas: The Cloud Forest People

One of the last tribes the Inca conquered was the Chachapoya, who are sometimes referred to as the "cloud forest people" because they lived in a mist-covered region of northern Peru. Relatively little is known about them because their homeland was so remote and isolated. The ruins of their communities, including towns, houses, and ceremonial centers, show a distinctive style of circular stone construction. The most spectacular site is a mighty fortress called Kuelap, which sits on a ridge overlooking the Utcubamba River.

Spaniards Arrive

Francisco Pizarro, a Spanish conquistador (conqueror), led a group of soldiers into Peru in 1532. By this time, Huáscar was dead and Atahualpa was emperor. The Spaniards had fewer than 180 men and Atahualpa had thousands of troops, so the Spaniards made a plan to ambush the Inca leader in order to conquer his people. Pizarro invited Atahualpa to meet him in the town of Cajamarca, in northern Peru, but when the Inca emperor arrived, no one appeared to greet him. Eventually, a Spanish priest approached, a Bible in hand. Atahualpa looked at it, having never seen a book before. He then threw it on the ground, and the Spaniards emerged from their hiding places and captured him. The Spaniards demanded a huge ransom of gold and silver for Atahualpa's release, but when it was delivered, they killed him instead of letting him go.

Pizarro knew he could claim the Inca Empire only if he took Cusco, the capital and most sacred Inca city. Unlike the Inca, the Spaniards had horses and steel weapons, which enabled them to seize control of Cusco in August 1533. The Spaniards were amazed at the city's wealth, and they helped themselves to its treasures. Pizarro agreed that Manco, one of Huayna Capac's sons, should become the new Inca leader, although he would have no real power.

Francisco Pizarro led the Spanish conquest of Peru. Here, he heads through the Andes Mountains to Cajamarca, where he met Atahualpa.

Pizarro gave Spaniards grants of land on which to settle. To work the land, the conquistadores enslaved the indigenous people under a system known as the *encomienda*. In the encomienda system, Spaniards were supposed to teach the Inca Christianity in exchange for their labor.

Manco soon understood that the Spaniards planned to stay. He gathered his troops together and rebelled. He would battle the Spaniards for years.

Diego de Almagro, Pizarro's partner in the expedition to Peru, had helped lead the Spaniards to victory in Cusco. Later, the two men could not agree on how to divide the empire between them, and Pizarro and his brothers arranged Almagro's murder. Three years later, in 1541, supporters of Almagro murdered Pizarro.

Meanwhile, Manco continued to fight the Spaniards. They eventually killed him, but his son and, later, his grandson continued the battle. In 1572, the Inca resistance was finally crushed, and Manco's grandson Tupac Amaru, the last Inca leader, was put to death.

Pizarro (center) stands in a plaza in Cusco. The Spanish conquered the Inca capital in 1533.

Colonial Peru

Francisco de Toledo, viceroy of Peru from 1569 to 1581, laid the foundations of the Spanish colony. He organized it to fulfill the needs and greed of the Spanish conquerors and the Spanish king. Toledo extended the encomienda and built on the mita

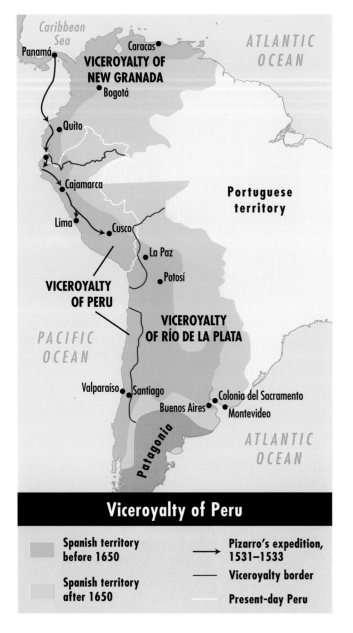

Caribbean Sea

ATLANTIC OCEAN

Panamá

Caracas

VICEROYALTY OF NEW GRANADA

Bogotá

Quito

Cajamarca

Portuguese territory

Lima

Cusco

La Paz

Potosí

VICEROYALTY OF PERU

VICEROYALTY OF RÍO DE LA PLATA

PACIFIC OCEAN

Valparaíso

Santiago

Colonia del Sacramento

Buenos Aires

Montevideo

ATLANTIC OCEAN

Patagonia

Viceroyalty of Peru

Spanish territory before 1650

Spanish territory after 1650

→ Pizarro's expedition, 1531–1533

— Viceroyalty border

— Present-day Peru

tax system of the Inca. The Spaniards used local chiefs as officials to collect taxes. They forced indigenous people to pay their taxes by working in mines and textile workshops or on the land.

The number of indigenous people in Peru dropped in the 16th and 17th centuries. Many thousands died of overwork, and even more died from diseases such as smallpox brought by the Europeans. Smallpox had long existed in Europe, so Europeans' bodies had developed an immunity to it. The disease would make them sick, but it would usually not kill them. The indigenous people had never before been exposed to smallpox, however, so it spread quickly, wiping out entire communities.

During the colonial era, the Spaniards divided into two groups: *peninsulares*, who had been born in Spain, and *criollos*, who were born in the colonies. The peninsulares ruled the colonies, much to the frustration of the criollos. Meanwhile, many Spanish men had children with indigenous women, so Peru had a growing population of *mestizos*, people of both indigenous and European descent.

By the 1700s, the Viceroyalty of Peru covered most of western South America. Lima was its capital. The city flourished from taxes on trade goods, which passed through the city on the way to Spain.

Toward the end of the century, indigenous people, tired and frustrated with the taxes and exploitation, rebelled against Spanish rule. Their leader was a mestizo named Tupac Amaru II, who claimed to be descended from Tupac Amaru, the last Inca ruler. The Spanish crushed the revolt, and in 1781, Tupac Amaru, like his namesake, was executed in Cusco's main plaza.

José de San Martín led the fight for Peruvian independence.

Independence

In the early 19th century, many South American colonies revolted against Spain and became independent, but Peru remained loyal to Spain. But many indigenous, mestizo, and criollo Peruvians resented Spanish rule. The peninsulares treated the criollos like inferiors. Few criollos held high positions, and taxes and restrictions hurt their farming and trading activities.

The movement for independence gained momentum when General José de San Martín, a criollo from Argentina, arrived in Peru in 1819. The general had freed his own country and helped Chile gain independence. Now, he was eager to see Peru do the same. Following a successful attack on Lima, San Martín declared Peru's independence on July 28, 1821.

But Spain's supporters fought back. In 1822, General Simón Bolívar, who had liberated Venezuela and Colombia, intervened. Bolívar met with San Martín, but the two generals were at odds. Bolívar wanted the people to elect the government, while San Martín favored rule by a king. No one knows what they said at their meeting, but after it was over San Martín left for Chile and soon moved to France. Bolívar, with General Antonio José de Sucre of Venezuela, went on to secure Peruvian independence by defeating Spanish forces in 1824.

In the early years after independence, many different people held power in Peru. In fact, a total of 35 presidents ruled between 1825 and 1865. The country also united with Bolivia in the Peru-Bolivia Confederation in 1836, but it lasted just three years.

The Guano Boom

In the mid-1800s, guano—bird droppings used as fertilizer—became the mainstay of Peru's economy. Indigenous people usually did the dirty job of digging for guano, although some Chinese immigrants also collected guano. The first guano shipment reached Europe in 1841. British and French companies controlled the guano industry, and the Peruvian government made money by imposing heavy taxes on them. By the 1860s, the guano boom accounted for more than 80 percent of the nation's income. But by the 1870s, many rich guano deposits had run out, and the companies found cheaper

The Highest Railroad

Peru used some of the money from the guano boom to fund the Peruvian Central Railway, which connects Lima, the coastal capital city, with La Oroya, a mining center in the highlands. An American named Henry Meiggs directed the early construction, engineering a remarkable system of tunnels, bridges, and zigzags to take the railway line up the mountains. The route required digging a tunnel through the Andes at an elevation of 15,693 feet (4,783 m). Disease killed thousands of workers during the construction, which began in 1870. The railroad was the world's highest for many years, but a railway connecting China and Tibet now holds that record.

guano alternatives elsewhere. This proved disastrous for the Peruvian economy.

Nitrates and the War of the Pacific

With the collapse of the guano industry in the late 1870s, the Peruvian government was unable to pay its debts and faced bankruptcy. Nitrates, which were used to make fertilizer and explosives, had been discovered in the Atacama Desert on the border between Bolivia and Chile. Both countries claimed ownership of the region. Peru backed Bolivia and tried to negotiate a settlement, but the negotiations failed, and in 1879, Chile declared war on Peru and Bolivia. Chile won the war, and under the Treaty of Ancón in 1883 gained land from both countries. In 1929, Chile returned part of the Atacama territory to Peru.

Into the 20th Century

At the end of the 19th century, a small, wealthy elite continued to dominate Peruvian society. The economy was largely under foreign control, first by British companies, which by then owned the railways, and then by North Americans, who had extensive mining interests in Peru.

In 1908, Augusto Leguía y Salcedo was elected president and began a series of reforms. He expanded education and started a program of public works—building roads, bridges, and railroads funded by banks in the United States—and he gave rights to explore oil fields to the International Petroleum Company, a U.S. company. Leguía regained the presidency in 1919 and became a dictator. He was ruthless in suppressing opposition, and the military finally forced him from power in 1930.

In 1924, Víctor Raúl Haya de la Torre formed the American Popular Revolutionary Alliance (APRA) to represent the interests of the middle and working classes. APRA was especially concerned with improving conditions for indigenous people and ending foreign control of Peru's major industries. Haya de la Torre ran for president in 1931 but lost. Some APRA supporters claimed that the elections had not been fair. Sugar workers in Trujillo rose up in protest, and the army killed more than 1,000 APRA supporters. The government arrested Haya de la Torre, and he was not freed until 1933.

In 1945, José Luis Bustamante y Rivero, backed by several liberal political parties including APRA, became president.

Bustamante improved freedom of the press, changed the constitution to limit presidential power, and tried to enact other reforms.

Military Rule

In 1948, General Manuel Odría overthrew Bustamante. He became a dictator, outlawing opposition and suppressing criticism in newspapers. In the following years, Peru would continue to swing between democratically elected governments and military rule. In the 1960s, democratically elected president Fernando Belaúnde Terry began road projects and improved social programs, but the price of goods began to skyrocket, and in 1968, the military ousted him.

Fernando Belaúnde Terry

Fernando Belaúnde Terry (1912–2002) was born into an upper-middle-class Peruvian family in 1912. He spent most of his early life abroad, being educated in France and the United States. After becoming an architect, he returned to Peru in 1936. His political career began in 1945, when he entered Congress. He spent many years opposing the dictatorship of Manuel Odría before founding the Popular Action Party in 1956. He was twice elected president, in 1968 and 1980. Although his years in office were marked by economic instability and increased violence by rebel groups, he was widely respected for upholding democratic government and for his development projects.

The 1968 military coup was a turning point in Peru's history. Most military governments tend to be right wing, limiting freedoms and keeping power in the hands of the wealthy, but this military government proposed many social and economic reforms. Under General Juan Velasco Alvarado, the government took over many large international companies. It broke up large plantations and turned them into cooperative farms, where many farmers would work the land together. It also helped people in the cities by limiting the cost of basic goods. Wealthy landowners and businesspeople challenged these reforms. Meanwhile, inflation continued to rise, the government was deeply in debt, and many people lacked jobs.

Economic Chaos and Rebel Groups

A democratic election was finally held again in 1980, and voters returned Fernando Belaúnde to office. He faced immense problems. The economy was failing. Peru was growing much of the world's supply of coca, which is used to make the illegal drug cocaine. The United States was pressing Peru to do something about it, but many indigenous farmers relied on coca for their survival. Meanwhile, rebel groups called the Shining Path and the Tupac Amaru Revolutionary Movement (MRTA in

A Piece of the Amazon

For many years, Peru and its neighbor Ecuador disputed ownership of an area of the Amazon forest. The region has pristine forests, deep ravines, and mountains often shrouded in fog. It is known to have rich deposits of uranium, gold, oil, and other natural resources. The conflict had led to war between the two countries in 1941, 1981, and 1995. Finally, the two nations signed a treaty agreeing to the border in 1998.

Spanish) were active in the highlands. These groups used violent attacks and assassinations to try to overthrow the government. Belaúnde sent security forces to the highlands to put down the rebellion. Hundreds of people were killed, and as many as 2,000 more disappeared and were likely murdered.

Members of the Shining Path train in 1987. The Shining Path wanted Peru to become communist. Under communism, the government controls the economy and owns all businesses.

In 1985, Alan García Pérez was the first member of APRA to be elected president. He tried to introduce the economic reforms that APRA had long promoted, including cutting taxes and refusing to repay more than 10 percent of Peru's international debts, but this led to economic chaos. Inflation skyrocketed, reaching an annual rate of 7,690 percent in 1990. This inflation rate means that something that cost 1 sol (the basic unit of Peruvian money at the time) at the beginning of the year would cost 769 soles at the end of the year.

Meanwhile, the rebel groups had taken over parts of the highlands and were sometimes threatening Lima. Finally, in the early 1990s, leaders of both rebel groups were captured. The groups no longer appeared to be a threat until December 1996, when the MRTA attacked the Japanese ambassador's residence in Lima and took almost 500 people hostage. Peruvian soldiers eventually ended the siege, killing all the rebels.

President Alberto Fujimori instituted a series of reforms known as Fujishock. The changes were meant to control inflation and stabilize the economy.

The Fujimori Decade

In 1990, Alberto Fujimori won the presidential election, defeating the renowned writer Mario Vargas Llosa. The son of Japanese immigrants, Fujimori was a university teacher with almost no political party backing, but many Peruvians were tired of the traditional Peruvian establishment and wanted to try something new.

Fujimori enacted drastic economic reforms, limiting the amount of money the government spent and ending price controls on many goods. During this same period, the rebel leaders were captured, and the end of their violent attacks increased his popularity. Fujimori claimed that Congress was preventing him from implementing other reforms, and in 1992, he closed Congress and suspended the constitution.

Despite these moves, Fujimori easily won the 1995 presidential election. By this time, Congress was again open and was cooperating with Fujimori. This enabled him to introduce more radical economic reforms, such as returning government-owned industries to private ownership. Peru's economy grew steadily during the second half of the 1990s.

Fujimori was reelected in 2000, but many people did not accept the election result because Peru's constitution limits presidents to two terms. Then, just weeks after the election, a high government official was caught on videotape bribing a congressperson to support Fujimori. The president's popular support collapsed, and he soon fled to Japan. In 2007, he was tried and convicted of corruption and sentenced to six years in prison. He was also accused of serious human rights abuses.

Recent Times

In 2001, Alejandro Toledo became the nation's first president of indigenous descent. With half the nation living in poverty, he promised to help people in need and root out corruption. But Toledo was unable to live up to his promises.

Although many Peruvians continue to struggle, the economy has been strong and stable in recent years. This gives Peruvians hope that with their long tradition of working together, their nation will be able to meet future challenges.

Alejandro Toledo served as president from 2001 to 2006. As president, he worked to reduce poverty and increase trade.

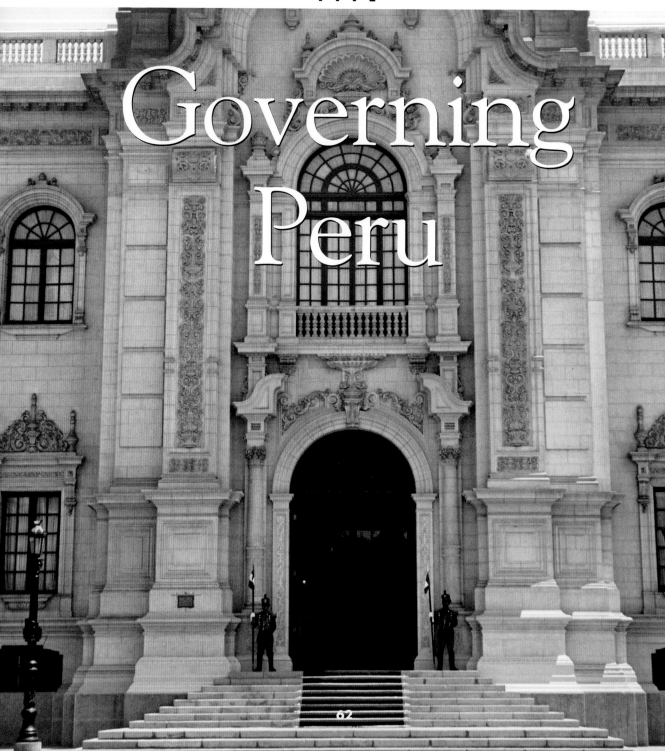

Governing Peru

P ERU IS A REPUBLIC, A NATION IN WHICH THE PEOPLE CON-
trol the government. It is also a representative democracy, a
system in which people choose others to represent their interests in the government. Peru's first constitution was written
in 1827. Its 15th and present constitution went into effect in
1993. It lays out the basic structure and rules of government.
According to Peru's constitution, the government is organized
into three branches—executive, legislative, and judicial.

Opposite: **The presidential palace is located in the Plaza Mayor in Lima.**

Alan García Pérez

President Alan García Pérez (1949–) was elected to Peru's highest office twice, first in 1985 and

again in 2006. García was born into a political family. His father was involved with the American Popular Revolutionary Alliance (APRA), and in 1976 García joined the party. He progressed swiftly. He won a seat in Congress in 1980 and then became secretary-general of APRA before being elected president at age 36. Never before had an APRA candidate won the presidency, and many Peruvians were optimistic because of García's youth and energy.

But during García's presidency, the economy collapsed and violent rebel activity grew. He lost the 1990 presidential election.

After a decade living abroad, García returned to Peru in 2001. In 2006, he ran for president again, promising to strengthen the economy and advance rights for women. He was elected with 53 percent of the vote.

The Executive Branch

The president of Peru is directly elected by the people, and everyone ages 18 to 70 is required to vote. The president is the head of the executive branch. He or she is elected for a five-year term and can serve two terms in a row. Peruvians also elect two vice presidents.

The president appoints a prime minister, who is the top adviser. With the prime minister's advice, the president selects the rest of the Council of Ministers, each of whom is in charge of a different field, such as education, agriculture, and the economy.

NATIONAL GOVERNMENT OF PERU

Executive Branch

PRESIDENT

FIRST VICE PRESIDENT

PRIME MINISTER

SECOND VICE PRESIDENT

COUNCIL OF MINISTERS

Legislative Branch

CONGRESS
(120 REPRESENTATIVES)

Judicial Branch

SUPREME COURTS

CONSTITUTIONAL COURTS

SUPERIOR COURTS

COURTS OF FIRST INSTANCE

The 1993 constitution, which was written after President Alberto Fujimori closed Congress in 1992, gives the president greater power than previous constitutions. It says that if the president dissolves Congress, he or she has the power to rule by decree, meaning that the president can make laws without the approval of any other individual or group.

The 120 members of the Peruvian Congress meet in the Legislative Palace in Lima.

The Legislative Branch

Peru has a one-house Congress with 120 members elected to five-year terms. Candidates for Congress must be Peruvian citizens at least 25 years old. The Congress passes laws and approves the government budget and treaties.

Former president Alberto Fujimori (left) stands trial before justices of the Peruvian Supreme Court.

The Judicial Branch

The Supreme Court of Justice is the highest court in Peru. It includes 16 judges. Below the Supreme Court are 28 Superior Courts, each of which reviews cases in one judicial district. Courts of First Instance (trial courts) are located in each province. The judges in all these courts are appointed by the National Council of the Judiciary. Leaders in the legal profession and university presidents elect the council's seven members to five-year terms.

Peru also has a Constitutional Court, which has seven members elected by Congress to five-year terms. The role of the Constitutional Court is to ensure that the constitution is upheld.

The National Flag

Peru's flag was adopted in 1825. It has three equal vertical stripes. The one in the center is white and the other two are red. In the middle of the white stripe is the national coat of arms. In the top left corner is a vicuña, which represents Peru's wealth of wildlife. In the top right is a cinchona tree, the source of quinine, which is used to treat malaria. The tree represents Peru's wealth of plants. And across the bottom are golden coins, symbolizing Peru's wealth of minerals. Above the coat of arms is a green wreath framed by branches of palm and laurel tied at the bottom with a red and white ribbon.

Local Government

Peru is divided into 25 regions, which are subdivided into provinces, which are in turn made up of districts. Lima doesn't belong to any region. Instead, it is its own province. Voters in each region elect government officials who plan regional development and public investment projects, promote economic activities, and manage public property. A mayor and a city council govern Lima.

Peruvian electoral officials count votes during the 2006 presidential election.

Lima: Did You Know This?

Lima, the capital of Peru, is also Peru's largest city by far, with a population of 8,472,935 in 2007. Conquistador Francisco Pizarro founded the city in 1535, and it became the capital of the Viceroyalty of Peru in 1543. Lima prospered as a trade center during the 17th century, and after Peru proclaimed its independence in 1821, Lima became the nation's capital.

Today, Lima is Peru's financial, industrial, political, and cultural center. The city has a mix of architectural styles. Many buildings in the old city center, including

San Francisco Convent and the Cathedral of Lima, date to the colonial period. In contrast, the financial district has towering skyscrapers.

Lima is home to the National University of San Marcos, which is the oldest university in the Americas. It was established in 1551. The city also has many fine museums, including the Museum of Natural History and the Museum of the Nation (above).

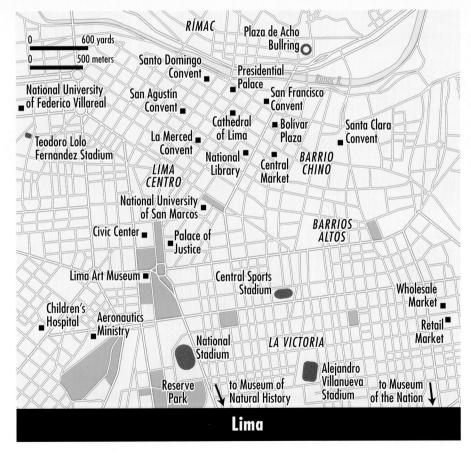

RÍMAC

Plaza de Acho
Bullring

0   600 yards
0   500 meters

Santo Domingo
Convent

Presidential
Palace

Rímac R.

National University
of Federico Villareal

San Agustín
Convent

San Francisco
Convent

Cathedral
of Lima

Bolívar
Plaza

Santa Clara
Convent

Teodoro Lolo
Fernandez Stadium

La Merced
Convent

National
Library

Central
Market

BARRIO
CHINO

LIMA
CENTRO

National University
of San Marcos

BARRIOS
ALTOS

Civic Center

Palace of
Justice

Lima Art Museum

Central Sports
Stadium

Wholesale
Market

Children's
Hospital

Aeronautics
Ministry

Retail
Market

National
Stadium

LA VICTORIA

Reserve
Park

to Museum of
Natural History

Alejandro
Villanueva
Stadium

to Museum
of the Nation

Lima

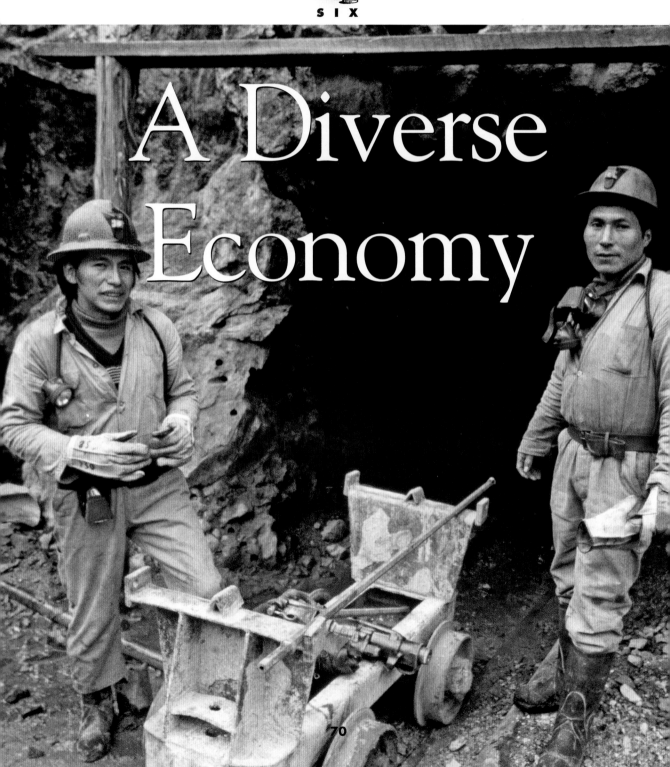

A Diverse Economy

I n Inca times, agriculture was the mainstay of Peru's economy. During the Spanish colonial era, mining and agriculture were both central. Then, in the 20th century, Peru developed more of its mineral resources, and then, in the 1960s, it became the world's leading fishing nation. Today, Peru's economy relies on all these activities and more.

Opposite: **Workers stand at the entrance to one of Peru's many silver mines. Peru is the world's second-largest silver producer.**

Birds circle a fishing boat along the southern coast of Peru. Fishing is a mainstay of Peru's economy.

Highland Farming

In the Andes, indigenous farmers work small plots of land, often on the slopes of mountains where it is impossible to use mechanized vehicles. Farmers still turn the soil with ox-drawn wooden plows. They sow seeds by hand and drain water down the hillsides to irrigate the fields. Crops grown at high altitudes include quinoa, *kiwicha*, and *kañiwa*, three nutritious

The Coca Plant

For centuries, people of the Andes have chewed a mixture of coca leaves, ash, and lime, which has a druglike effect that combats hunger and fatigue. Coca has long been traded in local markets, and some Andean people carry pouches especially for coca leaves.

Coca is also used to make the illegal drug cocaine, which sells for high prices around the world. The crop, which grows well on the eastern slopes of the Andes, is relatively easy to tend. Farmers can make much more money growing coca than they can growing coffee or cacao (the source of chocolate).

Peru has tried to control the coca trade by destroying coca plants and persuading farmers to grow other crops, but coca production continues to thrive. More than 200,000 people are still thought to work in the business in Peru.

grains that Peruvians have been cultivating for centuries. Highland farmers also grow corn, coffee, and potatoes, which originated in the Andes.

A farmer harvests potatoes on his plot in the Andean highlands. People have been cultivating potatoes in Peru for more than 8,000 years.

Coastal Farming

Large-scale farming takes place on the coast. The most fertile regions are the river valleys, but large areas of desert are now irrigated and produce crops such as sugarcane, potatoes, wheat, rice, cotton, corn, olives, and fruits and vegetables. In

A woman tends to her goats in the Sacred Valley of the Incas, north of Cusco.

2003, Peru was the world's second-largest producer of asparagus, after China. In the same year, asparagus became Peru's leading agricultural export, replacing coffee at the top spot. The coastal region also has many chicken farms, and many families keep pigs and goats.

Fishing is vital to Peru's economy. Peru has the second-largest catch of any country in the world, trailing only China. The largest catch is anchovies, which thrive in the cold Peru Current. Most of the anchovies are turned into fish meal and exported as animal feed. Peruvian fishers also catch bonito, mackerel, sea bass, tuna, swordfish, and other species. Most of this fish is sold in local markets.

Peru's vast Amazon forests contain valuable hardwoods, such as cedar and mahogany, and a small but growing industry in Peru supplies timber for furniture and plywood. In addition, people harvest rubber and cinchona (a source of quinine) from trees in the Amazon. Settlers and businesses also cut or burn trees to make clearings where they can farm and raise cattle.

What Peru Grows, Makes, and Mines

Agriculture (2006)

Sugarcane	7,600,000 metric tons
Potatoes	4,700,000 metric tons
Rice	2,200,000 metric tons

Manufacturing

Residual oil fuel (2005)	2,958,000 metric tons
Cement (2006)	5,000,000 metric tons
Animal feed (2001)	1,508,000 metric tons

Mining (2006)

Copper	1,050,000 metric tons
Iron ore	4,800,000 metric tons
Silver	3,471 metric tons

But many people have protested the destruction of the forests, limiting the development of a timber industry in Peru.

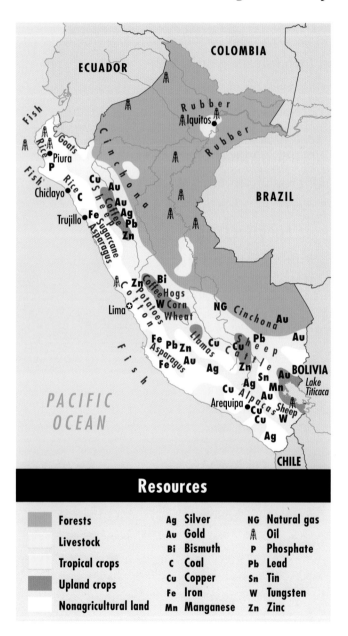

Resources

Forests	Ag	Silver	NG Natural gas
Livestock	Au	Gold	🛢 Oil
Tropical crops	Bi	Bismuth	P Phosphate
Upland crops	C	Coal	Pb Lead
Nonagricultural land	Cu	Copper	Sn Tin
	Fe	Iron	W Tungsten
	Mn	Manganese	Zn Zinc

Mining and Energy

Peru is rich in mineral resources. It is the site of South America's largest gold mine. It is also the world's second-largest silver producer and third-largest producer of copper and zinc. Copper, which is the nation's most valuable export, is mined on the southern coast. Among Peru's other mineral resources are bismuth, iron, lead, zinc, phosphate, and manganese.

Peru produces about 120,000 barrels of oil per day. Most of Peru's oil comes from the northern desert coast and from the waters near that coastline. Peru's Amazon region also has extensive reserves of oil and natural gas. Environmental and human rights groups have criticized Peru's government over plans to auction off swaths of the Amazon to oil and gas companies. They say that the amount of Peruvian Amazon territory open to oil exploration rose from 13 percent to 70 percent between 2005 and 2007.

The Interoceanic Highway

Many Peruvian presidents have dreamed about roads to link the remote parts of their vast country. In the 1940s, Manuel Odría pushed ahead with the Pan-American Highway, linking the major coastal cities. In the 1970s, Fernando Belaúnde promoted the Marginal Highway, linking Chiclayo on the coast with parts of the eastern Andes. Then, in the 2000s, Alejandro Toledo backed the idea of the Interoceanic Highway, which would be the first paved road to cross South America from east to west.

The highway, scheduled to be completed in 2011, stretches for 3,400 miles (5,500 km) from the Peruvian Pacific coast to São Paulo and Santos on the Atlantic coast of Brazil. The engineering challenges in building the road were enormous. It required one bridge 2,369 feet (722 m) long over the Madre de Dios River.

That's nearly a half mile (800 m) long! Other parts of the highway cross Andes Mountain passes at elevations of 13,000 feet (4000 m). The economy of towns along the highway is already booming. The road is intended to carry produce from the Amazon to large coastal towns so it can be shipped to Asian markets.

Dams have been built on many rivers flowing from the Andes. These dams produce hydroelectric power that provides about three-quarters of Peru's energy.

Industry

Most of Peru's manufacturing is in the Lima area. Factories there produce goods ranging from processed foods, animal feed, household machines, and clothing to fuel oil, steel, cement, fertilizer, and chemicals. Cars and other vehicles are assembled in Peru. Meanwhile, countless self-employed people and families produce goods in small, independent workshops.

Chefs prepare food for customers at a restaurant in Lima. About three-quarters of Peruvians work in service industries.

Tourism

Many Peruvians work in tourism, Peru's fastest-growing industry. They are employed by hotels or restaurants, drive taxis, or work as guides. The number of foreign visitors to Peru increased by over 60 percent between 2000 and 2008 to about 2 million. Many want to see Machu Picchu, South America's leading tourist destination, but Peru has many

Money Facts

The *nuevo sol* ("new sol") is Peru's basic monetary unit. One new sol is divided into 100 *céntimos*. Peru issues coins of 1, 5, 10, 20, and 50 céntimos and 1 sol. Paper notes come in denominations of 10, 20, 50, and 100 soles. In 2009, 3.26 new soles was equal to US$1.

Most of Peru's paper money depicts historical figures, including José Abelardo Quiñones Gonzáles (a military aviator), Raúl Porras Barranechea (a writer and politician), and Jorge Basadre Grohmann (a historian).

other attractions for visitors. Travelers head to the coast and highlands to visit archaeological sites and museums. The Amazon is popular with ecotourists, who want to see its plants and wildlife without harming the environment. Those seeking more adventure go rock climbing or white-water rafting.

Machu Picchu is one of the most popular tourist sites in Peru. More than 400,000 people visit it every year.

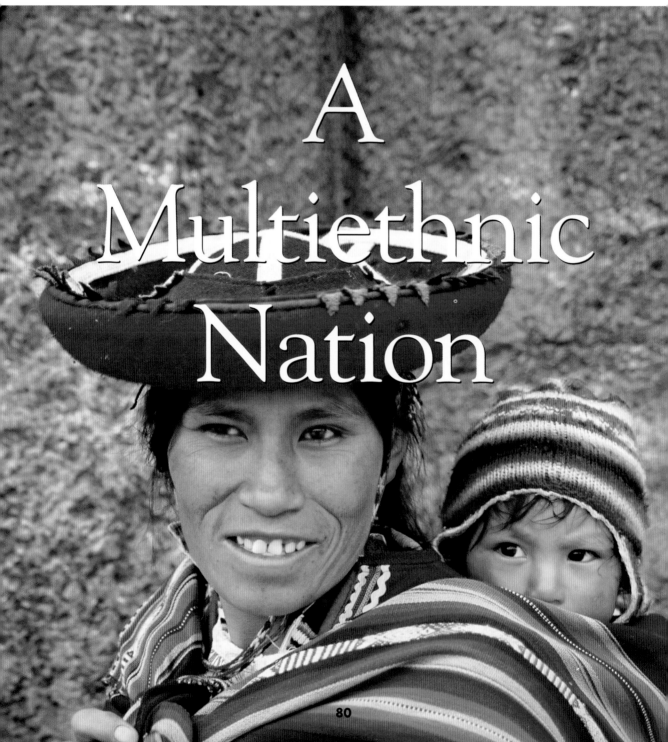

A
Multiethnic
Nation

IN RECENT DECADES, MANY PERUVIANS HAVE MOVED FROM rural areas to cities, looking for jobs and a better education for their families. As a result, more than 75 percent of Peruvians now live in cities. Ninety-five percent of the people live on the coast or in the highlands, while just 5 percent live in the vast Amazon forest east of the Andes.

Most major cities are on or near the coast. This includes Lima, the capital and largest city, which is home to more than a quarter of all Peruvians. The only large cities in the highlands are Cusco and Huancayo, and in the Amazon, Iquitos is the single major city.

Opposite: **A woman and her child wear traditional Peruvian clothing.**

People in traditional and modern dress mingle on the busy streets of Puno, a city in southeastern Peru.

Population of Major Cities (2007)

Lima	8,472,935
Arequipa	749,291
Trujillo	682,834
Chiclayo	524,442
Piura	377,496

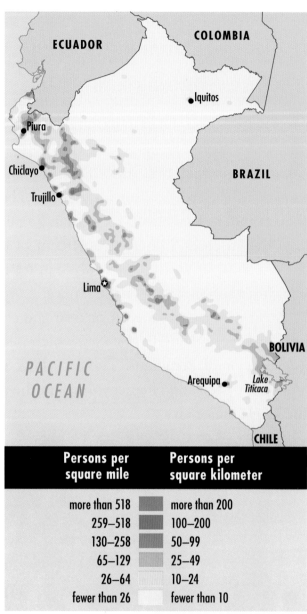

Above: **Many Quechua people live in the Peruvian highlands.**

Persons per square mile		Persons per square kilometer
more than 518		more than 200
259–518		100–200
130–258		50–99
65–129		25–49
26–64		10–24
fewer than 26		fewer than 10

Indigenous Peoples

Nearly half the population of Peru are indigenous, or Native, Peruvians. With the exception of its neighbor, Bolivia, Peru has the highest proportion of indigenous peoples of any country in South America.

The largest indigenous group in Peru is the Quechua, who live everywhere in the highlands except around Lake Titicaca. The Quechua are divided into many different culture groups, but they all speak a version of the Quechua language. Most are farmers or herders. At the higher mountain elevations, the Quechua raise llamas and alpacas and grow potatoes, quinoa, and a few other crops. At lower altitudes, their main crops are corn and coca.

Who Lives in Peru?

Indigenous people	45%
Mestizos	37%
European Peruvians	15%
Afro-Peruvians, Asian Peruvians, and others	3%

A Quechua woman tends a llama while carrying her child.

Another large indigenous group, the Aymara, lives in the altiplano around Lake Titicaca. The altiplano is a cold, barren place where it is difficult to grow crops and there is little pasture for animals. It is the poorest part of Peru, and many Aymara have a hard life.

Life on the "Floating Islands"

Some Aymara people live on "floating islands" made from totora reeds, which grow in swamps around Lake Titicaca. The Aymara make thick mats from the reeds and float the mats on the lake. They anchor these "islands" to the bottom of the lake so they don't move around. Every few months, the Aymara add reeds to the top of the island as the reeds on the bottom rot away. The Aymara also use totora reeds to build homes, boats, and even a school and a chapel. Most men on the floating islands earn a living by fishing or working on the mainland. Women make weavings and trinkets to sell to the many tourists who visit each year.

Dozens of different indigenous tribes live in the Peruvian Amazon. Until the 19th century, few outsiders had contact with these groups.

The forest tribes build houses of palm wood and leaves. Their main crop is cassava, a white root vegetable similar to the potato. They also hunt, though nowadays more often with a gun than with the traditional bow and arrow. Many women wear a *cushma*, an ankle-length tunic with holes for the head and arms. They weave cushmas from wild cotton. Indigenous peoples of the forest paint their bodies with dyes made from plants.

An indigenous man plays a flute in the Peruvian Amazon.

A Multiethnic Nation **85**

Medicinal plants are among the many types of goods available at markets in the Amazon.

The Ashaninka, Machiguenga, Piro, Shipibo, Conibo, and Amahuaca are all tribes of the montaña. Most have contact with mestizo communities in the region, and some have elementary schools and a medical center. Some Shipibo travel to Iquitos and Pucallpa to sell their pottery and cloth, which are decorated with geometric patterns. They also sell jewelry they make with beads and glass.

The Nahua, Matsés, Yagua, and Huitoto are some of the groups who live in the low-lying Amazon rain forest. They live close to rivers and rely on canoes to get around. They have a strong belief in the spirit world around them and hold frequent religious festivals. At these times, they paint their bodies with lavish designs and dance for hours to the music of flutes and drums.

About 11,000 Achuar people also live in the Amazon. Their land sits atop extensive oil reserves. The activities of the oil companies have harmed the land and water, and the Achuar have been compensated.

Mestizos

Mestizos, people of mixed indigenous and European heritage, make up about one-third of Peru's population. Most are middle class or working class. Some have professional or managerial jobs. They might work as teachers, lawyers, doctors, civil servants, or politicians. Others run businesses, work in TV, or write for newspapers.

A salesman shows off an electronic embroidery machine at a textile convention in Lima. Many middle-class people in Peru are mestizo.

Peru's Cowboys

The Morochuco, a mestizo group, live on the plains near the city of Ayacucho. Many Morochuco raise cattle, and they are renowned for their skills with horses. Children are accomplished horseback riders from an early age, and women join men galloping across the flatland to catch bulls. Morochuco men wear long, dark-colored ponchos over brightly colored, thick woolen tights and sandals. Women ride astride in their full skirts.

For centuries, the Morochuco were seminomadic. They wandered across the land with their animals. The Morochuco had a reputation for strength and bravery and fought alongside Simón Bolívar in the wars of independence.

Many working-class mestizos do manual labor and need more than one job to get by. Men may work on construction sites and drive taxis or do gardening part-time. Many women work as maids while also running the family home. Many mestizo families have stalls on city streets and in markets, where they sell everything from religious trinkets to designer clothing.

European Peruvians

People of European descent make up about 15 percent of the population of Peru. Some are the descendants of Peru's original Spanish settlers. Peru's Spanish families have traditionally been wealthy landowners, businesspeople, politicians, and military leaders. Despite their relatively small number, they have had great influence in the country.

After Peru became independent, other European immigrants arrived from countries such as Germany, France, Italy, and England. Some settled in Lima, where they became involved in business and industry, while others opted for more remote parts of the country. In the 1850s, a group of immigrants from Austria and Prussia (which is now part of Germany) established farming communities in the high forest of the eastern Andes. They built wooden houses with sloping roofs typical of their homelands. Today, some of these houses still stand, and many of the communities' inhabitants still speak German and dance traditional German folk dances such as the polka.

Afro-Peruvian dancers perform at an event in Washington, D.C. Many Peruvian dances have roots in Africa.

Afro-Peruvians

Fewer enslaved Africans were brought to Peru than to other parts of South America. They arrived first in the 16th century, to work as servants in Spanish households. Later, many enslaved Africans worked on coastal sugar and cotton plantations. Slavery was abolished in Peru in 1854, but the former slaves had neither education nor money, so they continued to struggle. Today, Afro-Peruvians live mainly in and around Lima, in some southern coastal towns such as Cañete and Chincha, and on the northern coast in Piura and Lambayeque. Many work as laborers or farmhands.

Asian Peruvians

Asians have been moving to Peru since the middle of the 19th century, when Chinese immigrants began arriving to work in the guano industry or on the Peruvian Central Railway. Today, Lima has a large Chinese community, and in cities throughout Peru, Chinese families run successful businesses, shops, and restaurants. Altogether, ethnic Chinese in Peru total about 200,000.

Peru has the second-largest population of people of Japanese descent in Latin America, after Brazil. Most arrived in the early 20th century, and today the community numbers about 100,000.

Two men enjoy lunch at a restaurant in Lima's Chinatown neighborhood. Peru is home to the largest Chinese community in South America.

How Do You Say...?

English	Spanish	Quechua
How old are you?	¿Cuántos años tienes?	Jaiq'a watayoq kanki?
Where do you live?	¿Dónde vives?	Maypin tiyanki?
I am sick.	Estoy enfermo.	Onq'osianin.
Where do you come from, sir?	¿De dónde vienen, señor?	Maymantataq kanki taytay?
I'm from the United States.	Yo soy de los Estados Unidos.	Estados Unidos mantan kani.

Languages of Peru

Spanish and Quechua are the official languages of Peru. About 84 percent of Peruvians speak Spanish, and about 13 percent speak Quechua. There are 30 to 40 different dialects, or versions, of Quechua, which makes it difficult for people from different regions to communicate. People in the Lake Titicaca region speak Aymara, and the forest tribes have their own languages.

The Spanish alphabet has 28 letters. Consonants sound similar to those in English. The differences are that Spanish does not have the letter *k* or *w* but does include the letters *ch*, as in "chair"; *ll*, which sounds like the "y" in "yacht"; *ñ*, like the first *n* in "onion"; and *rr*, a long, vibrating *r*.

A man in Lima reads a Spanish language newspaper.

Most Quechua letters are pronounced similarly to Spanish. In addition to letters, the Quechua language includes an apostrophe, which indicates a sharp clicking sound. In Quechua words, the next to the last syllable is usually accented.

Peruvian schoolchildren line up for a field trip.

Education

Peru is considered to have one of the best education systems in Latin America. About 88 percent of adult Peruvians can read and write. Education is free, and by law, all children ages six to fifteen must attend school. However, about 25 percent of Peru's children do not complete primary (elementary) school, and only about 50 percent of children go on to secondary school.

Many families move from rural areas to towns because they want a better education for their children. Schools in towns have better equipment, more and better-qualified teachers, and generally higher standards than schools in the countryside. In the cities, classes are often large, and students in many schools attend in shifts of morning and afternoon sessions.

In some rural areas, people live far from schools. There is little public transportation, so children walk many miles every day to attend classes. A school built of totora reeds now stands on one of the floating islands in Lake Titicaca, and children from many villages travel by boat to get there. Although Spanish is the principal language used in schools, rural children sometimes receive lessons in their indigenous languages, particularly Quechua, an official language of Peru. In the lowlands, some schools specialize in teaching children of indigenous Amazonian communities, who also have their own languages.

The National University of San Marcos in Lima, founded in 1551, is the oldest university in the Americas. Other large towns in Peru also have universities and colleges. Students can take courses in many disciplines, including arts, sciences, law, medicine, business, and languages.

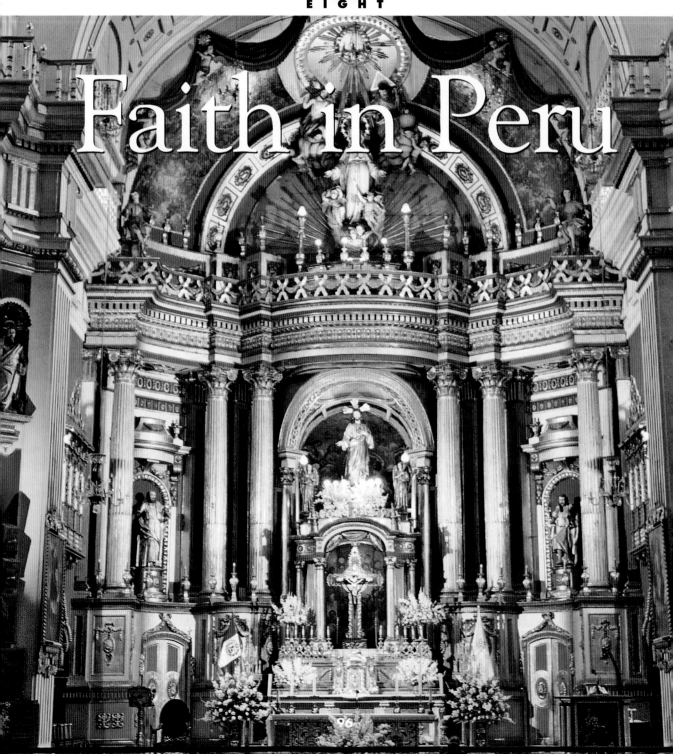

Faith in Peru

F

RANCISCO PIZARRO ESTABLISHED HIS FIRST TOEHOLD IN Peru's northern desert on a spot he called San Miguel de Piura. It was there, about 500 years ago, that Spaniards built Peru's first Catholic altar and held its first mass. Pizarro and the many Spanish priests who followed him over the next hundred years carried the Catholic message to many parts of Peru. They tried to convince, or sometimes force, the indigenous peoples to give up their own beliefs and adopt Christianity.

Opposite: **The altar of Saint Peter's Church in Lima is covered in gold leaf.**

A missionary priest prays as the Spanish prepare to execute Atahualpa, the last Inca king of Peru.

Religions of Peru (2003 est.)

Roman Catholicism	81%
Seventh-Day Adventism	1.4%
Other Christian religion	0.7%
Other, unspecified, or none	16.3%

Faith in Peru **97**

What resulted was a mixture. Although most Peruvians are officially Roman Catholic, many still hold strongly to indigenous beliefs. Often, Catholicism and indigenous religion merge. This mixing of religions is called syncretism.

The Catholic Church

Peru has no official religion, but more than 80 percent of Peruvians are Catholic. The country is filled with churches, ranging from grand cathedrals in bustling cities to adobe mud churches in Andean villages to simple wooden churches in jungle settlements.

Catholicism is the most common religion in Peru. This small Catholic church is in the village of Taray.

Two Saints

Saint Rose of Lima was the first Catholic saint born in the Americas. She was born Isabel Flores de Oliva in Lima on April 20, 1586. After a short life in which she devoted herself to prayer and helping the sick and the hungry, she died on August 30, 1617. Pope Clement X declared her a saint in 1671. Today, she is the patron saint of Peru. Many Catholics visit her shrine in Lima, and today people across the nation celebrate August 30, her feast day, as a national holiday.

Martín de Porres was born in Lima in 1579, the son of a woman of African descent and a Spanish nobleman who was later the governor of Panama. Martín grew up in humble surroundings. Throughout his life, he devoted himself to caring for the poor and the sick. By the time he died in 1639, he was known across Lima for his spiritual devotion and skill with animals. In 1962, Pope John XXIII named Martín de Porres a saint. He was the first black saint in the Americas.

Men in the city of Ica carry a statue of Jesus through the streets. Religious processions are common in Peru.

In Peru, the calendar is filled with Catholic festivals. Some honor saints and other holy figures, such as Saint Rose of Lima. One of the largest festivals in all the highlands is the procession of the Lord of the Earthquakes in Cusco, which takes place on the Monday of Holy Week, the last week before Easter. This tradition dates back to 1650, when an earthquake severely damaged many churches. A statue of Jesus said to have miraculous powers was carried through the streets, and the earthquake shocks soon subsided. Since then, the statue, known as the Lord of the Earthquakes, has become Cusco's patron saint.

An even larger procession, held in Lima each October, dates back to an earthquake in 1655. Despite the massive destruction in the coastal region, a painting of Jesus on the wall of a hut survived. The painting—the work of an enslaved African—later survived another earthquake and became a legend. Known as the Lord of the Miracles, it was paraded around Lima each year. After the original painting was destroyed by fire in 1923, a replica was made. The procession, which draws up to 2 million people, combines elements of Catholic tradition with African and indigenous religions. It is South America's largest religious procession.

Women carry incense as they join in Lima's Lord of the Miracles procession.

Other Religions

Peru allows people of all religions to practice their faiths freely. Today, there are significant numbers of Baptists, Seventh-Day Adventists, Mormons, Buddhists, and Hindus. There are small Jewish communities in Lima and Cusco, and Muslim communities in Lima and Tacna.

Peru is home to people of many different religions. Here, members of the Hare Krishna sect, an offshoot of Hinduism, walk through a plaza in Lima.

The Inca built many temples to the Sun, including this one at Machu Picchu.

Indigenous Religions

Long ago, Peruvian civilizations built large temples and pyramids on Peru's desert coast to honor their gods. In Cusco, the greatest Inca shrine was the Temple of the Sun. An 8-inch (20 cm) band of gold stretched around the entire building at roof level, and the walls were lined with sheets of beaten gold. Inside was a large gold image of the sun.

Men in traditional dress participate in Inti Raymi, the Festival of the Sun. This Inca festival takes place on the winter solstice, the shortest day of the year in the Southern Hemisphere.

Peru's indigenous peoples worship many gods, including gods of the sun, thunder, lightning, and the earth and its waters. Hills, mountains, and some stones have spiritual significance, too. In the Andes, the night sky is brilliant with stars, planets, and streaking meteorites, and Andean peoples long revered them as part of their spiritual world.

Indigenous religions feature many kinds of spirits, some good and some evil. Offerings of coca leaves and sacrifices of llamas were made at certain times of the year to keep the spirits happy or to keep away bad luck.

Some of these beliefs survive to the present day and are felt most strongly in communities in the countryside. Village shamans, or wise men, offer comfort in times of need. They are believed to have the power to cure illness and to ease problems. Central to their ceremonies is a *mesa*, or table, upon which a variety of small ritual objects such as seashells, seeds, animal skins, colored sweets, and miniature crosses are set. The shaman "reads" the objects to help solve problems.

Some shamans, or healers, use wild plants to help treat illnesses.

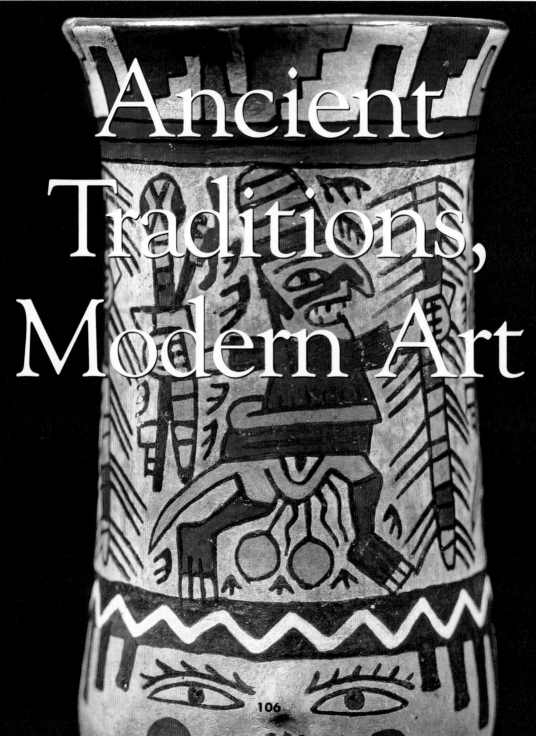

Ancient Traditions, Modern Art

The Moche culture is noted for its painted ceramics, such as this bottle shaped like a fish.

S OME OF PERU'S ARTISTIC TRADITIONS DATE BACK THOU-sands of years. Peru's ancient peoples produced some of the finest weaving the world has known. They used natural dyes to color the thread and wove geometric designs or images of animals and birds into the cloth.

They made similar designs on pottery. Some of the best examples came from the Nazca and Moche cultures. The Nazca often made animals and birds, while the Moche made pots shaped like human faces. They also depicted everyday scenes, such as war and medical operations. The Moche and others also created masks, jewelry, *tumis* (ceremonial knives), and much more out of gold. Tombs at Sipán and Sicán have revealed hundreds of items made of gold, silver, copper, and other metals.

Opposite: **This vase from the Nazca culture was made between 1,400 and 2,200 years ago.**

The National Museum

The National Museum, located in Lima, contains a magnificent survey of all Peru's ancient civilizations. Exhibits include models of many Inca sites around Cusco and other archaeological sites. The museum also features a comprehensive review of traditional dress from around the country and displays that show life before the arrival of the Spanish.

Crafts

Peru's weaving tradition continues to the present day. Among Quechua families, weavings are often used for clothing or for sale in local markets. Women spin yarn out of cotton or llama, alpaca, or sheep's wool while they tend their animals.

A woman weaves cloth from alpaca wool.

Weavings have distinctive colors and designs, often related to a particular village or place. The patterns and symbols represent the natural world, ancient traditions, and local stories as well as modern objects such as trains and planes.

Other handicrafts in Peru include wood carving and making jewelry of gold, silver, and semiprecious stones. People in Pucara, in the highlands, make decorated clay bulls, which symbolize the Spanish influence in the country. Huancayo is renowned for its carved gourds, while artisans in Ayacucho make *retablos*, small wooden altars with carved religious and everyday scenes.

Marcos Zapata made a painting of the Last Supper in 1753. In it, he portrayed Jesus and his disciples preparing to dine on a guinea pig.

Art

Art during the colonial period was largely restricted to religious paintings. Many colonial artists came from Spain and Italy, but a native Peruvian type of painting known as the Cusco school emerged in the 17th and 18th centuries. Diego Quispe Tito (1611–1681), who was descended from an Inca family, was the leader of this movement. He and others made richly decorated carvings and colorful paintings with religious themes. Marcos Zapata made a painting in Cusco's cathedral showing Jesus at the Last Supper with a guinea pig—a local delicacy—as the main course.

Paintings from the early 19th century tended to glorify the events of Peru's colonial history. In the 20th century, Peruvian artists such as José Sabogal (1888–1956), influenced by the social content of the great artists in Mexico, identified with Peru's indigenous peoples. Many modern Peruvian artists, including painter Fernando de Szyszlo and sculptor Joaquin Roca Rey, create abstract art, using color and shape in compositions rather than carefully reproducing the way something looks.

The Inca had no written language. Much of what we know about them comes from the writings of 16th-century Spanish writers, such as Inca Garcilaso de la Vega and Felipe Guaman Poma de Ayala. After Peru gained independence, Peru's most popular writer was Ricardo Palma (1833–1919), whose entertaining stories combine history and fiction. This style was in sharp contrast to the deep thinking of philosopher and writer José Carlos Mariátegui (1895–1930) and journalist and novelist Clorinda Matto de Turner (1852–1909). Matto de Turner was the first woman editor of a daily newspaper in the Americas. She denounced corruption in the government and the church and supported equal rights for indigenous peoples. Her ideas were considered so controversial that she was forced to leave Peru, and she spent her last years in Argentina.

Manuel González Prada (1844–1918) was another writer who focused on the plight of indigenous peoples. He was part of the *indigenista* movement, which sought to improve their

Taking Pictures

Mario Testino is a world-class photographer. He was born in Lima in 1954 and has lived in London since 1976. Testino works mainly in the fields of fashion and celebrity photography, and he has photographed members of the British royal family. His images of Great Britain's Princess Diana taken shortly before her death in 1997 were used by newspapers and magazines throughout the world.

Mario Vargas Llosa

Mario Vargas Llosa (1936–) is one of the greatest writers of his generation. His work has been acclaimed since the publication of his first novels, *The Time of the Hero* and *The Green House*, written in the 1960s. He has worked in many different styles, from experimental to lightly comic. But regardless of the style, many of his works deal with people's struggle for freedom.

In some of his novels, like *Aunt Julia and the Scriptwriter* (1977), he has looked to his own life for inspiration. Other novels focus on historic events. *The War of the End of the World* (1981) centers on a local military conflict in Brazil in the 19th century, while *The Feast of the Goat* (2000) is based on Rafael Trujillo, the dictator in the Dominican Republic who was assassinated in 1961.

Like many writers in Latin America, Vargas Llosa has also been involved in politics. Initially a supporter of communism, he gradually moved toward the political center. In 1990, he ran for president as part of a center-right group but lost to Alberto Fujimori. He now devotes most of his time to writing and lecturing.

lives. In his novel *Broad and Alien Is the World*, Ciro Alegría (1909–1967) looked to the APRA party for solutions. Native Peruvians and their way of life were also central to the work of José María Arguedas (1911–1969), a mestizo who was brought up in a Quechua community.

During the second half of the 20th century, writers moved away from themes that focused on indigenous peoples and rural areas. Cities—especially Lima—provided a new background. Among the most important of these writers are Mario Vargas Llosa, Julio Ramón Ribeyro, and Alfredo Bryce Echenique, who wrote the popular satire of Lima's upper and middle classes *A World for Julius*.

The panpipe is an ancient instrument. It is the ancestor of the harmonica.

Music and Dance

Among the traditional elements featured in Andean music are panpipes, a flutelike instrument made from reeds. Other typical Andean instruments are drums, *charangos* (small, guitarlike instruments built into armadillo shells), and conch shell trumpets. Spaniards introduced harps, violins, and guitars to Peru.

The most common highland dance is the *huayno*, which is performed to melancholy love songs that can be heard everywhere in Peru—on the radio, in public squares, as background market music. Couples dance it with a vigorous stamping of feet. *Criollo* music, which developed on the coast, has its origins in Spanish and African rhythms. The most popular criollo dance is Peru's national *marinera*, a graceful courtship dance.

Opera Star

Juan Diego Flórez (1973–) is an opera singer, who was born in Lima, where his father was a noted guitarist and singer. Flórez was only 23 when he made his debut at La Scala, the world-renowned opera house in Milan, Italy. Since then, he has had major roles in opera houses around the world and has been hailed as the heir to Luciano Pavarotti, a great Italian tenor. In 2007, he was awarded Peru's highest decoration, the Gran Cruz de la Orden del Sol del Peru, and he has also appeared on the country's 2-sol stamp in a series honoring contemporary Peruvian musicians. Both are rare honors for someone so young.

Afro-Peruvian Revival

Chabuca Granda (1920–1983), whose real name was María Isabel Granda Larco, became a singer and composer when it was not considered a proper career choice for a young woman, so she disguised her name. Early in her career, she produced criollo waltzes influenced by the romantic beauty of Barranco, one of Lima's suburbs, with its French-style houses and large gardens. From this era came what is perhaps her best-known composition, "La Flor de la Canela" ("Cinnamon Flower"), which has become an anthem for the city of Lima. Later, she incorporated Afro-Peruvian rhythms into her waltzes.

One of her songs, "Maria Lando," gave Susana Baca de la Colina (1944–) (left) her breakthrough in North America in 1995. Susana Baca is a singer of Afro-Peruvian descent who has been at the forefront of the revival of Afro-Peruvian music in Peru. Her band uses instruments such as the *cajón* (a wooden box on which the player sits and thumps out a rhythm), the *guapeo* (a clay pot), and the *quijada* (the jawbone of a donkey), as well as guitar and bass. She and her husband run an institute dedicated to the collection, preservation, and creation of Afro-Peruvian culture.

Peruvian students and their visiting American pen pals enjoy a game of soccer in the Amazon.

Sports

Soccer is by far the most popular sport in Peru, both to play and to watch. Children use any patch of spare ground to kick a ball around, while tens of thousands of spectators watch matches between teams that play every week during the season in most Peruvian cities.

The Great Nene

Most people regard the soccer player Teófilo "Nene" Cubillas as Peru's greatest athlete. He was born into a humble family in Lima in 1949. He was always a fan of the Alianza Lima soccer team and first played for it in 1966, when he was only 16 years old. Two years later, he joined the Peruvian national team. In 1970, he scored five goals in four games in the World Cup, soccer's most prestigious tournament. By the end of his career, Cubillas had played in 513 games and scored 303 goals. During that time, he received only one yellow card for foul play.

Peruvians are passionate about bullfighting, and many families enjoy visiting the bullring during their vacations. Lima's Plaza de Acho is the oldest bullring in the Americas.

With its long coast and magnificent waves, it is not surprising that many Peruvians enjoy surfing. In fact, the coast of Peru has been the location for numerous surfing world championships. The coast also offers opportunities for other water sports such as swimming and diving, while the mountains offer endless challenges for climbers, hikers, and walkers.

The beach in Lima's Miraflores district draws crowds of people looking to swim or simply enjoy the sunshine.

Living in Peru

A family reunion in the mountains of Peru

F AMILY LIFE IS CENTRAL TO PEOPLE IN PERU, AND OFTEN several generations live under the same roof. In many families, both parents work outside the home and grandparents help look after young children.

The Extended Family

Peruvian families celebrate important events together, such as birthdays, baptisms, first communions, marriages, anniversaries, and graduations. The extended family, which includes godparents and friends, gets together to sing, dance, and eat. Godparents are important members of the extended family. They not only help their godchildren with money or advice, but they also maintain a special relationship with the parents, understanding that they will help each other if the need arises.

Opposite: **In Peru, young and old often gather for family celebrations and other events.**

Men work together building an adobe house in the mountains of Peru.

Extended families are especially important in indigenous communities. Some of these communities are based on an extended family unit, or *ayllu*, a way of life that dates back to the Inca. All members of an ayllu help one another with work such as building homes and plowing, sowing, and gathering the harvest.

Peruvian Family Names

Peruvians use two family names. Take, for example, a man named Juan Flores Álvarez and his sister María Flores Álvarez. Flores is their father's paternal name, and Álvarez is their mother's paternal name. If María marries Juan García Benavides, she traditionally keeps her own name and becomes María Flores Álvarez de García. For practical reasons, however, many women drop their mother's paternal name (here, Álvarez), and in that case, María would become María Flores de García. Their children will take their father's and mother's paternal names, so a son might be Jorge García Flores and a daughter, Rosa García Flores. Many men use only the first of their two family names, so Juan Flores Álvarez might call himself simply Juan Flores.

Most Peruvian families in the cities live in high-rise apartment buildings. Because families often have two or three children, children usually share bedrooms. Most cities in Peru are surrounded by shantytowns, where people arriving from rural areas quickly build dwellings. About half of Lima's people live in shantytowns. A small number of Peruvians are very wealthy and live in luxurious houses. They have large gardens, employ servants, and send their children abroad for schooling.

Many Quechua and Aymara still follow a centuries-old lifestyle in the highlands. Traditional Quechua and Aymara

The elegant home in Cusco features ornate balconies.

National Holidays in Peru

New Year's Day	January 1
Maundy Thursday	March or April
Good Friday	March or April
Labor Day	May 1
Saint Peter's and Saint Paul's Day	June 29
Independence Day	July 28
National Day	July 29
Saint Rose of Lima Day	August 30
Battle of Angamos	October 8
All Saints' Day	November 1
Immaculate Conception	December 8
Christmas	December 25

homes are made of adobe mud-brick or stone with roofs of tile or thatch made from tough mountain grasses. Inside, families sleep on a wooden bed with a mattress of split reeds and covered with sheepskins and blankets. People cook over an open fire built on a platform inside the hut, or in a clay oven outside. In some places, one- and two-story brick houses with tiled roofs and windows are replacing adobe houses. These have interior rooms that more closely resemble rooms in a typical North American home.

Many Quechua homes are made of adobe. Bundles of grass form the roofs.

Traditional Dress

Many younger indigenous men and women prefer to wear typical western clothes such as jeans and sweaters, but some Quechua and Aymara still wear traditional dress, especially at festivals. For women, this means full skirts, or *polleras*, gathered at the waist and worn over several petticoats. They wear woolen jackets called *juyunas*, which are decorated with buttons, under a shoulder cloth usually fastened at the front by a pin. An *aguayo* or *k'eperina*, a large shawl for carrying babies, market produce, or even animals, is slung across the back. The most distinctive items of women's clothing are hats. Aymara women wear bowler hats, hard felt hats with a round top. Among Quechua communities, there is a wide variety of hat style, color, and decoration, so much so that it is often possible to tell which village a woman comes from by looking at her hat.

For work, indigenous men wear knee-length trousers and roughly woven shirts, a wide woven belt called a *chumpi*, and sandals, usually made of rubber from old tires. Their hats

A young girl wears a blend of modern and traditional clothing.

Young people relax in a plaza in Cusco. Most Peruvians dress much the same as people in North America.

vary from felt sombreros to knitted hats with earflaps, or *chullos*, which are sometimes decorated with beads and tassels. Sometimes, because of the cold, men wear both hats at the same time. At fiesta time, men sometimes wear lavishly decorated vests. At all times, men and boys wear a poncho. Among the Quechua, ponchos often have bright stripes and a distinctive pattern that relates to their village.

Haircutting Ceremony

Some Peruvian traditions have come down through the generations from Inca times. One ceremony for young children is still followed in parts of the Andes. Friends and family gather for a child's first haircut. The child is dressed in simple clothes, and each adult may cut a lock of hair. Each visitor presents the child with a gift, usually a small sum of money, which is put aside for later years.

Foods of Peru

In Peru's cold highlands, soups and stews are by far the most popular foods. Depending on what families grow, everything goes into them—fresh or dried meat, corn, carrots, beans, many kinds of potatoes, and hot peppers and spices, especially the very hot *ají*, a type of chile pepper. Guinea pigs, known locally as *cuy*, have long been an Andean delicacy. Today, indigenous people eat them fried or grilled, usually on special occasions. They are on the menu in many restaurants.

Arroz chaufa is a popular fried rice dish in Peru. Chinese immigrants introduced fried rice to Peru, adding typical Peruvian flavors.

Peruvians also eat chicken and duck. A favorite dish along the northern coast is *seco de cabrito* (baby goat) served with beans and rice. *Ají de gallina*, creamed chicken with hot peppers served over boiled potatoes, is another popular dish. Given Peru's long coastline, it is not surprising that fish is the basis of many Peruvian dishes. *Ceviche* is raw fish marinated in lime or lemon juice, onions, and hot peppers and served with sweet potatoes, cassava, or corn. *Escabeche de pescado* is fish with onions, hot green peppers, red peppers, prawns, eggs, olives, cheese, and cumin. Shrimps are served in a stew called *chupe de camarones*.

Fish—from large catfish to razor-toothed piranhas—are eaten everywhere in the Amazon, served boiled or grilled with rice or cassava. Bananas come with virtually every meal— fried, mashed, or grilled—and banana leaves are stuffed with fish or corn and baked. Peruvians eat many kinds of fruit, including papayas, pawpaws, mangoes, passion fruit, and custard apples.

Andean Potatoes

Potatoes were first grown in the Andes centuries ago, and they remain a staple in the Andean diet. Long ago, the Andean people found a way to preserve potatoes. First, they squeeze out all the moisture by stamping on them, and then they expose the potatoes to the hot daytime sun and freezing nighttime temperatures. The end result—dried potato—is known as *chuño*. Dried potatoes can be kept for many months and then revived by boiling them in hot water.

Andean potatoes come in all sizes, shapes, and colors, including yellow, white, purple, and red, and Peruvians have endless ways of cooking them. Potatoes can stand alone as *papa ocopa*—sliced, boiled, covered in peanut sauce, and served with rice, eggs, and olives. To make *yacu chupe* (green soup), cheese, garlic, eggs, onions, and herbs are added to a potato base. *Causa* is a cold casserole of yellow potatoes mixed with hot peppers and onions. Perhaps the most popular potato dish in the highlands and on the coast is *papa a la huancaína*—boiled potatoes topped with a spicy sauce of milk and cheese.

Staying in Touch

Radio and television have made a huge difference to people living in remote parts of Peru. Most households have a radio, and many have access to broadcast or cable TV, even if they do not own a TV set. Today, isolated communities can receive the latest news as it happens.

Newspapers and magazines are published in Lima and some other cities, but getting them to other parts of Peru every day has always been difficult, even with airplanes. Lima's *El Comercio*, the nation's leading newspaper, was founded in 1839. It has a circulation of only 150,000. Instead of buying newspapers, many people browse through pages displayed on clotheslines at newspaper stands.

Newspapers are an important source of information for the people of Peru.

Many people enjoy watching television, especially *telenovelas*, which are usually melodramatic stories that continue for weeks or months. Many telenovelas in Peru are imported from Mexico and Venezuela. Almost as popular are talk shows, comedy shows, cartoons, and films imported from the United States.

In mountainous regions, Peruvians sometimes use donkeys to help transport goods.

Getting from here to there in Peru has always been difficult. The mountains are a major barrier between the coast and the eastern forests. The Inca built roads; the Spanish introduced horses; and in the 19th century, work began on the world's highest railway. Roads have never been an easy way to get from one part of the country to another. Landslides and floods can easily wipe them out. The highest mountain passes are very narrow and rough, and often only sure-footed llamas, donkeys, and mules or people on foot or on bicycles can cope with them.

Playing Ligas

To play the game of *ligas*, you need an elastic band about 15 feet (4.5 m) long. Two children stand opposite each other with the elastic around their ankles, forming a rectangle. A third child jumps in and out of the rectangle, sometimes on just one leg, sometimes on both, and sometimes with legs crossed or with alternate jumps on each side of the rectangle. The jumps follow a pattern, and if you make a mistake, you are "out."

It was only with the first airplane flights in the 1920s that good transportation began in Peru. Today, a regular system of flights covers every part of the country. This has been vital in the Amazon, where in the past river travel was the only option. Now, paved roads such as the Interoceanic Highway provide access to the heart of the forest.

The Best of Peru

In the early 2000s, Peru had a booming tourist industry and a thriving economy. Yet Peru is also wealthy and successful in many other ways. It is a land of unparalleled richness in animal and plant life. It has soaring mountains, dramatic volcanoes, lush forests, and grand deserts. And it has a proud Inca heritage, strong indigenous communities, and families committed to each other.

Peru boasts many fantastic landscapes. Here, hikers enjoy a walk through the Andes Mountains.

Timeline

Peruvian History

Farm people live in valleys of western Peru.	3000 BCE
The Chavín civilization reaches its peak.	900 BCE
The Nazca culture flourishes on Peru's southern coast.	100 BCE–500 CE
The Moche rule the northern coast of Peru.	100–700 CE
Much of Peru comes under the influence of the Huari.	700–1000
Chimú people create an empire in northern Peru.	1000–1438
Inca people begin an empire in southern Peru.	1200
The Inca Empire reaches its peak.	1438–1533
Spaniard Francisco Pizarro arrives in Peru.	1532
Pizarro founds Lima.	1535
The National University of San Marcos, the oldest university in the Americas, is founded in Lima.	1551

World History

c. 3000 BCE	Forms of writing are invented in China, India, and Sumeria.
c. 2500 BCE	Egyptians build pyramids in Giza.
c. 563 BCE	The Buddha is born in India.
c. 469 BCE	Socrates is born in Greece.
313 CE	Roman emperor Constantine recognizes Christianity.
610	The Prophet Muhammad begins preaching Islam.
618–907	The Tang Dynasty rules China.
1206–1227	Genghis Khan rules the Mongol Empire.
1215	King John of England agrees to the Magna Carta.
1300s	The Renaissance begins in Italy.
1400s	The Inca flourish in the Andes, and the Aztec thrive in what is now Mexico.
1464	The Songhay Empire is established in West Africa.
1492	Christopher Columbus arrives in the Americas.
1502	Enslaved Africans are first brought to the Americas.
1517	The Protestant Reformation begins.

Peruvian History

Spaniards crush a rebellion led by Tupac Amaru II.	1781
José de San Martín declares Peru independent of Spain but fighting continues.	1821
Peru wins independence.	1824
Chile declares war on Peru and Bolivia over the Atacama Desert.	1879
Víctor Raúl Haya de la Torre founds the American Popular Revolutionary Alliance (APRA).	1924
General Juan Velasco Alvarado seizes control of the government in a coup; Quechua is made one of Peru's official languages.	1968
The first APRA government takes office under President Alan García Pérez.	1985
Alberto Fujimori is elected president.	1990
Fujimori suspends Peru's constitution and dissolves Congress.	1992
Members of the Túpac Amaru Revolutionary Movement take almost 500 hostages in Lima.	1996
Alberto Fujimori is forced to resign.	2000
Alejandro Toledo becomes the first president of indigenous descent.	2001
Alan García is again elected president.	2006

World History

1776	Americans sign the Declaration of Independence.
1804	Haiti becomes independent following the only successful slave uprising in history.
1823	The United States announces the Monroe Doctrine.
1861–1865	American Civil War
1914–1918	World War I
1917	The Bolshevik Revolution brings communism to Russia.
1929	A worldwide economic depression sets in.
1939–1945	World War II
1950s–1960s	African colonies win independence from European nations.
1957–1975	Vietnam War
1989	The cold war ends as communism crumbles in Eastern Europe.
1994	South Africa abolishes apartheid.
2001	Terrorists attack the World Trade Center in New York City and the Pentagon in Arlington, Virginia.
2004	A tsunami in the Indian Ocean destroys coastlines in Africa, India, and Southeast Asia.
2008	The United States elects its first African American president.

Fast Facts

Official name: Republic of Peru

Capital: Lima

Official languages: Spanish and Quechua

Official religion: Roman Catholicism

Lima

Peru's flag

Adobe home

Year of founding:	1821
Founders:	José de San Martín, Simón Bolívar
National anthem:	"We Are Free, Let Us Always Be So"
Government:	Republic
Chief of state:	President
Head of government:	President
Area:	496,222 square miles (1,285,209 sq km)
Greatest distance north to south:	1,225 miles (1,971 km)
Greatest distance east to west:	854 miles (1,374 km)
Latitude and longitude of geographic center:	10° South, 76° West
Land and water borders:	Ecuador to the north, Colombia to the northeast, Brazil to the east, Bolivia to the southeast, Chile to the south, and the Pacific Ocean to the west
Highest elevation:	Mount Huascarán, 22,205 feet (6,768 m) above sea level
Lowest elevation:	Sea level, along the Pacific Coast

Average high temperatures:

	January	July
Lima	82°F (28°C)	66°F (19°C)
Cusco	68°F (20°C)	70°F (21°C)
Iquitos	90°F (32°C)	88°F (31°C)

Highest annual precipitation:	More than 100 inches (250 cm), in Iquitos
Lowest annual precipitation:	Less than 1 inch (2.5 cm), in Lima

Inca walls

National population (2008 est.): 29,180,899

Population of largest cities (2007 est.):

Lima	8,472,935
Arequipa	749,291
Trujillo	682,834
Chiclayo	524,442
Piura	377,496

Famous landmarks:
- ▶ *Colca Canyon,* Chivay
- ▶ *Inca walls,* Cusco
- ▶ *Machu Picchu,* Cusco
- ▶ *Nazca Lines,* Nazca
- ▶ *Chan Chan,* Trujillo
- ▶ *Tambopata-Candamo Reserve,* Puerto Maldonado

Industry: Peru is one of the world's leading producers of copper, silver, and zinc. Iron ore, lead, and petroleum are other major mining products. Peru's main manufactured goods include animal feed, petroleum products such as residual fuel oil, cement, steel, and sugar. Automobiles and appliances are assembled in Peruvian factories from imported parts. Peru has the second-largest fishing catch of any country in the world, and its major agricultural products include sugarcane, potatoes, rice, asparagus, and coffee. Many Peruvians work in services such as tourism, the nation's fastest-growing industry.

Currency: The nuevo sol ("new sol") is Peru's basic monetary unit. In 2009, 3.26 nuevo soles equaled US$1.

System of weights and measures: Metric system

Currency

Schoolchildren

Mario Vargas Llosa

Literacy rate (2007 est.):	88%

Common Spanish words and phrases:

adiós	good-bye
buenos días	good morning
buenas noches	good evening/good night
¿cuánto?	how much?
¿cuántos?	how many?
¿Dónde está . . . ?	Where is . . . ?
por favor	please
gracias	thank you
sí	yes
no	no

Famous Peruvians:

Susana Baca de la Colina *Singer*	(1944–)
Chabuca Granda (María Isabel Granda Larco) *Singer and composer*	(1920–1983)
Teófilo "Nene" Cubillas *Soccer player*	(1949–)
Alan García Pérez *President*	(1949–)
Clorinda Matto de Turner *Journalist*	(1852–1909)
Ricardo Palma *Writer*	(1833–1919)
Diego Quispe Tito *Artist*	(1611–1681)
Fernando de Szyszlo *Painter*	(1925–)
Tupac Amaru *Inca leader*	(?–1572)
Mario Vargas Llosa *Writer*	(1936–)

To Find Out More

Nonfiction

▶ Castner, James L. *River Life*. New York: Benchmark Books, 2002.

▶ Gruber, Beth. *National Geographic Investigates Ancient Inca: Archaeology Unlocks the Secrets of the Inca's Past*. Washington, D.C.: National Geographic, 2007.

▶ Steele, Philip. *Step into the Inca World*. London: Southwater, 2006.

Web Sites

▶ **CIA World Factbook: Peru**
www.cia.gov/library/
publications/the-world-factbook/
geos/pe.html
For facts and statistics on Peru's geography, history, people, government, and economy.

▶ **Cultures of the Andes**
www.andes.org/bookmark.html
For many links to sites on Andean subjects including music, history, archaeology, languages, and more.

► **National Geographic: Peru**
http://travel.nationalgeographic.
com/places/countries/country_
peru.html
*Includes videos, music, a photo gallery,
and more.*

► **Welcome to Peru**
www.peru.info/perueng.asp
*To find out more about Peru's history
and archaeology as well as tourist
information.*

Embassies

► **Embassy of Peru**
1700 Massachusetts Avenue NW
Washington, D.C. 20036
202-833-9860
www.embassy.org/embassies/pe.html

► **Embassy of Peru in Canada**
130 Albert Street, Suite 1901
Ottawa, Ontario K1P 5G4
Canada
613-238-1777
www.embassyofperu.ca/english.html

Index

Page numbers in *italics*
indicate illustrations.

Meet the Author

"I REMEMBER VIVIDLY MY FIRST VISIT TO PERU. MY TRIP BEGAN in Lima, the capital, and I was headed by bus for Lake Titicaca, the vivid jewel of the Andes Mountains," recalls Marion Morrison. At that time, Morrison had recently graduated from the University of Wales and was working with a United Nations project among the Aymara people. "The families were farming and herding beside the lake, and it was a dawn-to-dusk struggle for them to make a living."

The experience led to a lifelong interest in the people of the Americas, and she has since traveled to most countries in the hemisphere. Some, like Peru, have drawn her back time and

time again. "Peru has always had special fascination for me, with its overlay of European life on the ancient Inca culture. I lived in Cusco for some months when Tony, my husband, was filming for television."

Marion and Tony live in Great Britain in a house filled with books and photographs. Between travels, they keep in touch with Latin Americans in London. Morrison says, "In recent years, there has been an explosion of interest in Latin America with well-attended festivals, concerts, and exhibitions. News of upcoming events arrives every day.

Photo Credits